THE POWER
OF LIFE COACHING

VOLUME 4

MANIFESTING TRANSFORMATION IN FINANCIAL,
PROFESSIONAL, EMOTIONAL, SPIRITUAL,
WELLNESS AND
RELATIONSHIP ASPECTS

BY BARBARA WAINWRIGHT

IN COLLABORATION WITH

RICHARD BATTISTA, STEPHANIE RANDLE,
SHARON BARROWS COOPER, GLENN DEASON,
JILL SCHWARTZ, INGRID DUNHAM,
DR. LESIA CRUMPTON-YOUNG, JACQUELINE PIÑA,
CAROLYN SCOTT, GINGER PUREWAL,
MAE KILLEBREW-MOSLEY, DR. MELISSA TANNER,
PHIL CHABOT, STEFAN RUDOLPH, JAMES A. WHITE, SR.
GILDA SIMONET, MARY TRIMBLE, AND SIAN LINDEMANN

Books may be ordered through booksellers or by contacting:

Wainwright Global
www.WainwrightGlobal.com
1 (800) 711-4346

Because of the dynamic nature of the Internet, any web addresses or links contained in this book may have changed since publication and may no longer be valid. The views expressed in this work are solely those of the authors and do not necessarily reflect the views of the publisher, and the publisher hereby disclaims any responsibility for them.

The authors of this book do not dispense medical advice or prescribe the use of any technique as a form of treatment for physical, emotional, or medical problems without the advice of a physician, either directly or indirectly. The intent of the author is only to offer information of a general nature to help you in your quest for emotional and spiritual wellbeing. In the event you use any of the information in this book for yourself, which is your constitutional right, the author and the publisher assume no responsibility for your actions.

Print information available on the last page.

Scripture taken from the New King James Version®. Copyright © 1982 by Thomas Nelson. Used by permission. All rights reserved.

ISBN: 979-8-9912217-0-2 (sc)
ISBN: 979-8-9912217-1-9 (hc)
ISBN: 979-8-9912217-2-6 (e)

Library of Congress Pre-Assigned Control Number: 1-14141774271
Library of Congress Registration Number: TXu 2-443-960

Wainwright Global rev. date: 08/26/2024

Contents

Preface

In our fourth edition of The Power of Life Coaching Book, nineteen Certified Professional Coaches from Wainwright Global Institute of Professional Coaching, came together to share their coaching experiences with the world. We all have a passion for life coaching and appreciate the transformational experiences we have the privilege to share with each our clients. Each of us are motivated to provide excellent coaching services that result in men and women living an inspired life they love, a fulfilling life, because we help individuals to live from their heart, with passion.

The authors of this book, bare their souls, as they share their personal stories of struggle and their triumphs over them. Each life coach empowers their clients in their own special way. My hope is that you will feel a connection with each of these life coaches, and that you will be motivated to reach out to them for their services.

These life coaches provide life coaching services many different genres:

- Academic Coaching
- C-Level Executive Coaching
- Christian Life Coaching
- Clinical Health Coaching
- Grief Coaching
- Financial Coaching
- Health, Wellness and Healing Coaching
- Mind, Body, Spirit Coaching
- Mindfulness Coaching
- Personal Development Coaching
- Recovery Coaching
- Relationship Coaching
- Retirement Coaching
- Spiritual Coaching

My intention for creating this anthology book is to help you understand what life coaching is and the many different areas that life coaches can be of assistance in. There are over 52 coaching niches that Wainwright Global Certified Professional Life Coaches specialize in. So, whether you would appreciate improvements in your life, financially, professionally, spiritually, physically, emotionally, or in your relationships, a life coach can help you gain clarity of your best path and will encourage and motivate you to arrive at your divinely inspired destination.

I'd like to thank all the coaches that contributed to this book: Richard Battista, Stephanie Randle, Sharon Barrows Cooper, Glenn Deason, Jill Schwartz, Ingrid Dunham, Dr. Leslia Crumpton-Young, Jacqueline Piña, Carolyn Scott, Ginger Purewal, Mae Killebrew-Mosley, Dr. Melissa Tanner, Phil Chabot, Stefan Rudolph, James A. White, Sr., Gilda Simonet, Mary Trimble, and Sian Lindemann

I'd also like to thank my esteemed colleague and good friend, Gilda Simonét, for her much appreciated assistance with the creation of this book. I'd also like to say a special thanks Reigel Allen Munsayac for his artistry and help with the photos and covers for this book. And, also thanks to Don Salvador for his administrative help. It takes a lot of tenacity and dedication to create a book, or even a chapter in a book. I am grateful to all these professionals who made this book possible.

Harnessing the Power of Kaizen and Meditation in Coaching: A Transformative Journey

"Ultimately, the synthesis of Kaizen and Meditation in coaching embodies a whole-person approach to development that encompasses the mind, body, and spirit. By fusing these powerful methods, I can lead people to sustainable development and inner peace."

By Stephanie Randle

As a young child, I had a strong desire to help others. Whether it was family, friends, or others, I wanted to be there for them in whatever capacity they needed. This desire has always driven me to do whatever is possible to make those around me feel better during hard times. While in high school and college, this manifested itself through volunteering at a homeless shelter, mentoring and tutoring young people, and becoming a candy striper at the local hospital. Observing how grateful people were, simply by my presence during their time of need, changed something inside me forever. These gestures brought happiness into my life and showed me how much giving of myself can change someone's life. As I matured, so did this need to help others. As a result, I realized it was innately in me to dedicate the talents I possess to help others turn their aspirations into goals.

My coaching journey was not a direct one. Initially, my focus was solely on the success and profitability of my IT company. However, as I became more involved in managing the company, I realized the importance of coaching in business. This realization prompted me to provide business coaching and career development advice to my staff members. The results were overwhelming. Many of them went on to start their successful ventures, a testament to the transformative power of my mentorship. This success instilled a deep faith in coaching and inspired me to take my passion to the next level.

In 2019, I embarked on a new chapter in my career by establishing my coaching business in Business and Career Coaching. Armed with certifications and experience, I was well-prepared to help people unleash their potential. The year 2020 was a turning point that reaffirmed my commitment to coaching. In response to the increased levels of anxiety, stress, and uncertainty, I expanded my skill set and became certified as a Meditation Coach and Instructor. Today, I am proud to offer a unique blend of business and career coaching infused with the transformative power of meditation. My coaching practice is built on the pillars of my desire to help people and the proven benefits of Kaizen and Meditation in personal and professional development. This approach ensures that my clients receive the best support on their journey to self-improvement.

THE TRANSFORMATIVE POWER OF MEDITATION

Meditation is a practice that helps in maintaining mindfulness and calmness. I guide clients in finding their thoughts, emotions, and motivations through guided meditation. Equipped with techniques that bring awareness into daily life, people develop strength when faced with challenges and reduce anxiety while improving health. This clarity of mind helps one overcome obstacles with calm and awareness; hence, abilities are linked to emotional intelligence and self-awareness.

THE FOUNDATION OF KAIZEN IN COACHING

My journey recently led me to the profound principles of Kaizen. This Japanese philosophy is, in simple words, an approach focusing on small positive changes leading to continuous improvement. By ingesting the very essence of Kaizen into coaching sessions, I can help clients make little improvements that finally result in significant effects over the long term. This step-by-step approach involves breaking down significant goals into smaller ones and achieving those small steps over time. It builds a sense of progress and accomplishment, as the intense feeling of self-empowerment comes after one sees the materialization of their effort in real life. Incremental implementation of the principles of Kaizen during coaching acts as a continuous learning tool, an instrument for self-improvement, and a vehicle for transformation and achievement at both personal and collective levels.

THE SYNERGY OF KAIZEN AND MEDITATION

Combining Kaizen with meditation is potent for personal growth, productivity, and well-being. Kaizen's continuous improvement focus merges with the deep self-connection provided by meditation to derive unique benefits. When practiced daily, these two techniques could increase focus and clarity, innovation, long-term motivation and commitment, stress reduction, and well-being.

INCREASED FOCUS AND CLARITY: Meditation is the art of clearing the mind and focusing, which aids people in dealing with any task consciously and attentively. A Kaizen approach combined with such a focused mindset will help identify areas for improvement and implement small changes effectively.

PROMOTION OF INNOVATION: Through meditation, people learn to be creative and think out of the box since the mind is calm and has mental flexibility. When people meditate, especially practicing Kaizen, they become open-minded, curious, and ready to experiment, driving innovation in their personal and professional spheres.

SUSTAINED MOTIVATION AND COMMITMENT: Both Kaizen and Meditation teach people to keep pushing themselves forward and staying motivated toward their goals. Having real targets using the Kaizen method will help a person stay in touch with his inner drive, located inside through meditation, and pass through obstacles easily, always moving in growth.

STRESS REDUCTION AND WELL-BEING: Meditation has well-documented properties in reducing stress. Meditation is also used to soothe emotions. Now, combine the incremental progress mindset of Kaizen with meditation, and the person will face challenges with a more composed, resilient mindset and, hence, improved mental health and balance in life.

BALANCED GROWTH: These combined practices bring one to holistic growth: cognitive, emotional, and professional growth. This balanced way of growing gives sustainable development that is personally fulfilling and leads to value-based progress accompanied by a sense of purpose.

Although integrating Kaizen with Meditation fully provides a complete framework for self-development, mindfulness, and continuous improvement, the lessons learned from these two practices apply to all aspects of an individual's life. In my coaching, I try to balance these two practices and use Kaizen to help the client make small, incremental changes that can bring significant, long-term improvement. I also integrate meditation into this process to get a sense of calm and self-awareness to support the changes.

PRACTICAL APPLICATIONS IN COACHING SESSIONS

In my coaching sessions, I integrate Kaizen and Meditation in various ways to meet individual needs and objectives. For instance, I begin each session with a brief Meditation exercise to cultivate a calm and positive mindset for our work together. Clients are encouraged to apply Kaizen principles by setting small, achievable goals and regularly reviewing their progress. This practical approach ensures that the transformative power of Kaizen and Meditation is not just theoretical but a tangible part of their journey toward success.

THE IMPACT ON CLIENT SUCCESS

Combining Kaizen and Meditation has made my coaching very productive for my clients. Implementing these tools has lent much to their dramatic improvement in several areas, such as productivity and focus and a more profound sense of fulfillment. They said they felt empowered to overcome challenges, adapt to change, and pursue their goals confidently and clearly. This infusion of Kaizen and Meditation innovated their approach toward personal and professional growth by increasing self-awareness and well-being.

LOOKING AHEAD

Improvement does not end, and the limit to which positive changes brought about by these powerful techniques can be made is beyond the fantasy of one's imagination. By promoting Kaizen and mindfulness, I aim to create an environment where people feel inspired enough to realize their full potential, achieve goals, and live satisfied lives.

Ultimately, the synthesis of Kaizen and Meditation in coaching embodies a whole-person approach to development that encompasses the mind, body, and spirit. By fusing these powerful methods, I can lead people to sustainable development and inner peace.

What are some things you could do today that would allow you to fully develop yourself, achieve your goals, and live a richly rewarding life?

Stephanie Randle

About Stephanie Randle

Stephanie Randle is the President & Chief Executive Officer of Ignite Change (IC), a certified Business Strategist and Mindset Coach. Her unique approach, which involves creating customized plans for startups, businesses, executives, and individuals, sets her apart. This approach guides them in transitioning to reach their goals with clarity, purpose, and direction. With  over twenty years of coaching experience in the IT industry, Stephanie started her practice in 2019. She has also been a speaker at various events, delivering empowering talks on business topics specifically tailored for women entrepreneurs.

Stephanie is co-founder of Women and Girls Inspiring STEM Excellence (WISE), whose mission is to inspire black and brown women and girls to excel in STEM confidently to achieve and maintain success in their academic and professional lives.

Stephanie has a Master of Science in Technical Management and a Bachelor of Science in Computer Science. She also holds several technical and professional certifications.

Stephanie resides in Davidsonville, Maryland, with her family. For more information about Stephanie or to download her free meditation series Radiant Reflections: Empowering Meditations to Nurture Your Inner Light, go to ignitechangenow.com. Also, watch for Stephanie's forthcoming book, Unleashing Exceptional Leadership: The Power of Kaizen and Meditation for CEOs, available in September 2024.

From Divorce to Success: A Journey of Resilience and Transformation

"The key to success as a life coach is learning to ask the right questions. Most people already know the answers; when they repeat them, I simply move on."

by Richard Battista, MBA, CPC®

My life transformation started when my marriage began to deteriorate, as this tore me apart. Born and growing up in the United States of America in a well-educated and loving family in Boston, I had always aspired to be the best of what my youthful life was trained to be. In high school, the discipline and determination of an athlete were instilled in me, and to date, it has helped me a lot. However, while I was raised in such an environment, my personal life was about to be tested to the maximum.

The dissolution of my marriage brought with it a cascade of responsibilities and emotional turmoil. Arguably, that was not all because not only did I have to deal with the stresses that accompany the reality of being separated, but also being solely responsible for bringing up my four children. My ex-wife's battle with alcoholism translated to me being the sole custodian, and I walked down this unexpected route. She was a very caring person, and I did support her as much as I could.

Unfortunately, she passed on March 28, 2024, may her memories be a blessing.

During those challenging years, as I tried balancing both my career in the culinary industry and the demands of single parenthood, I discovered reserves of determination and resilience I never knew I had. Every day was a lesson in fortitude and prioritization, ensuring that my children received the love, support, and education they deserved. It was a period marked by sacrifice, but also by profound personal growth and a deepening understanding of the importance of empathy and compassion.

As a single parent, I was faced with the daily grind of juggling work and family. Mornings began before dawn, preparing breakfast and ensuring my children were ready for school. Every day was packed with after-school help with homework, continuation of activities, and getting ready for bed. In the middle of this, however, I maintained my career progression with the hopes of becoming a steady provider and caregiver for my children.

Before the trials of my personal life, my path had taken me through the rigors and challenges of military service. After high school graduation, I joined the US Army, serving in Vietnam for 14 months in the 1st Air Cavalry Division. Military life was one of the best formative periods of my life; I could never have given it a better description. During my service, I was faced with situations that tested my courage and leadership to the utmost. One particular encounter stands out in my memory. Amidst the dangers and chaos, I managed to save the lives of three of my men. Notably, this act of bravery earned me the Bronze Star Medal, which is the third-highest military decoration. I vividly recall the words of my commanding General of the 1ˢᵗ Air Cavalry Division: *"You are no better than anyone else, and no one is any better than you.*" This lesson in equality and humility became a cornerstone of my leadership philosophy. The military taught me the value of teamwork, discipline, and the importance of remaining calm under pressure- skills that proved invaluable in both my personal and professional life. These resonate with me during my coaching sessions since I am able to fit in the shoes of my clients and understand them better.

Amidst the turbulence of personal challenges and the foundational experiences of military service, my professional journey took a significant turn toward business coaching. This was not only a career transformation but, indeed, a progression of my passion for helping as many people as possible and changing their lives for the better. With a clear vision in mind and drawing on my extensive background in educational leadership, strategic business management, and culinary arts, I was able to establish the O2 Business Coaching LLC. This venture has capacitated me to channel my passion for mentoring into a formalized structure, guiding and empowering entrepreneurs, executives, and corporate leaders to navigate their challenges and achieve their full potential. The idea of business coaching resonated deeply with me, as it combined my passion for helping people with my extensive professional expertise. In my career path, I have found that the biggest difference between the people I started with in the early stages of my career and what they are doing now has to do with how great they were at learning. There is a world of new knowledge, opportunities, and relationships you can unlock if you let yourself.

Before venturing into business coaching, my career was deeply rooted in the educational and culinary arts sectors. Notably, I had the opportunity to lead the Professional

Culinary Institute, transforming it into a top-performing school which received global acclaim. This role required a blend of operational expertise, strategic vision, and a deep understanding of the culinary industry. In addition, the newly established La Brioche, a French Cuisine eatery, also provided me with ample experience in strategic development and business management. Growing the business to 15 restaurants and shops within five years and growing the multiple units' revenues by more than 40% were the major milestones that depicted my capability to drive growth and profitability in a competitive industry.

Amidst the chaos of my life, I was fortunate to meet and marry Susan, a wonderful woman from the Midwest. We have been married for nine years now, and she has been a grounding influence in my life. Susan brings important Midwestern values to our relationship, such as humility, kindness, and a strong work ethic. Her unwavering support and understanding have been instrumental in helping me navigate the challenges of my career and personal life. With Susan by my side, I have found a sense of balance and stability that allows me to continue pursuing my passion for coaching and helping others.

My approach to coaching is grounded in the belief that everyone can succeed, but sometimes, they need guidance and support to navigate challenges on their paths. At O2 Business Coaching LLC, I work closely with clients to develop tailored strategies that address their unique challenges and goals. Whether it's improving operational efficiency, enhancing leadership skills, or crafting a strategic growth plan, my coaching services are designed to provide practical, actionable insights that drive real results. My goal is to empower clients to take charge of their business and personal growth, helping them achieve sustainable success and fulfillment.

A cornerstone of my coaching practice is the emphasis on problem-solving skills. I am a firm believer that these skills are critical in the workspaces and are critical for roles full of uncertainties that involve dealing with complex issues. Problem-solving refers to identifying a particular challenge, coming up with possible solutions, analyzing those solutions, choosing the most appropriate solution, executing the solution, and reflecting on the solution. These steps are useful not only for solving current issues but also for building an organizational culture of continuous improvement and innovation. I follow the teachings of Marcus Aurelius, particularly from his book "Meditations." One of my favorite quotes is: "You have power over your mind - not outside events. Realize this, and you will find strength."

I help people develop the confidence to face uncertainties and turn obstacles into opportunities. In culinary leadership, I have come to an understanding that the secret to exceptional leadership is a powerful blend of speaking and listening. Listening is not passive; it is active engagement. It encompasses understanding, empathizing, and responding with intent. Practical steps to being a great listener include pausing and listening, asking open-ended questions, and reflecting and responding. To listen, you need to be present and to be present, you need to be conscious. Meditation for 20 minutes a day is key.

I have discovered that one of the keys to success as a life coach is learning to ask the right questions. In doing so, I have learned that most people already know the answers, and when they repeat them, I simply move on. For instance, I had a session with a man, and I asked how things were going. He indicated that he had a problem with his wife and his girlfriend and proceeded to explain the problem to me. So, my question to him was: Does your wife also have a boyfriend? He got very angry and indicated that there was no way he would stand for that. He then proceeded to say, "I know it's not right to be doing that," so my point here is that he knows it's not right to be doing what he's doing. There was no need for me to say anything further, and I just moved on. He had the answer!

Realization and Lessons

Several key lessons stand out upon reflecting on my transition to business coaching,

1.   Resilience and Adaptability: The ability to adapt and thrive amidst change is crucial for success. Embracing new opportunities and being open to learning and growth is essential for both personal and professional development. Life is full of unexpected turns. My experiences in Vietnam, the culinary industry, and my personal life have taught me the importance of resilience and adaptability.

2.   Empathy and Understanding: Effective coaching requires empathy and a genuine understanding of clients' challenges and aspirations. Building strong relationships based on trust and respect is fundamental to providing meaningful support and guidance.

3.   Continuous Learning and Growth: The biggest difference between those who succeed and those who don't is their ability to learn and adapt. Embrace new knowledge, opportunities, and relationships with an open mind. Transitioning into business coaching allowed me to align my personal experiences with my professional journey. Helping

others navigate challenges and achieve their goals became not just a career but a calling.

My journey from being drafted into the US Army, my turbulent marriage, and my transition from culinary leadership to business coaching has been a transformative experience that has been marked by empathy, resilience, and commitment to excellence. Notably, by leveraging my unique blend of culinary expertise and business acumen, I have been able to empower clients to achieve their full potential and navigate their paths to success. Through O2 Business Coaching LLC, I continue to inspire and uplift those I work with, helping them turn their aspirations into reality.

What step could you take today to transform adversity into opportunity and move closer to your goals?

About Richard Battista

Richard Battista is an award-winning entrepreneur, Vietnam veteran, and experienced leader in culinary arts and business coaching. With over 25 years of leadership in post-secondary proprietary school management and culinary entrepreneurship, Richard has a proven track record of transforming organizations

and empowering individuals. As the founder of O2 Business Coaching LLC, he provides strategic business coaching to entrepreneurs, executives, and corporate leaders. Richard is also a member of the prestigious Order of the Golden Toque and a dedicated life coach for veterans. I am a graduate of Burdett College with a degree in finance, a graduate of Northeastern University with a degree in management and social sciences and a graduate of Babson College with an MBA. I am also a Certified Professional Coach®. I pride myself on being a lifelong learner.

For more insights and a free valuable offer related to business coaching, visit https://www.o2businesscoach.com/ and sign up to receive exclusive tips and resources to help you unlock your full potential.

Use this QR Code to visit https://www.o2businesscoach.com/

You can find Richard Battista on LinkedIn here:

Linkedin.com/in/richard-battista-mba-cpc-89853244ba-cpc

Tools for Success

"Whether working with individuals, or groups and companies delivering custom workshops, I'm passionate about my clients' successes. I cannot be successful unless they are."

by Sharon Barrows Cooper

Dec 21, 1979, in Chicago, IL., my then husband came home from work, airline ticket in hand, advising me he didn't want to be married anymore & that I was going to my parents in NY. So, imagine being twenty-one, carrying your swaddled & blanketed 3-week-old son onto an airplane 4 days before Christmas on a cold windy day in Chicago. This was me. I checked 2 suitcases with all the baby accoutrements; (bottles, diapers, clothes, blankets, etc.), 2 tops, 2 pairs of jeans, and not one Christmas gift for my loved ones whom I'd see in a matter of hours. My heart & spirit felt wholly broken. I could only think about two things: first, the death of a marriage. Second, this little 6 ½ pound nugget of heavenly perfection. The most important thing that had ever happened to me, this little guy. He deserved all things great for his future; and I knew it was mine to set-up. (While this is my recollection & perspective, I recognize everyone in this accounting has theirs as well).

I boarded the aircraft, vaguely seeing the tall airline steward at the door, & proceeded to my seat near the back of the craft.

I was sniffling, and catching gulps of air in my throat, as the tears rolled incessantly. I was cradling my son; holding onto him as if the only protection he had in this entire world was me. Then from behind, I heard an upward inflectional, almost melodic questioning "Sharon?" I kept moving toward my seat, and heard it again, albeit a bit clearer and a tad louder, because I was paying attention now. "Sharon? What's the matter?" I turned around and realized the tall steward was a schoolmate from my childhood. "Biagio, hmph, snf, my husband, snf, doesn't want to be married anymore, and he's sent me home, snf, to my parents in NY."

Biagio immediately took my hand, reversed me, and walked me "back" toward the front of the craft. He seated me in a first-class seat, offered me a drink of water, and pinned plastic airline wings on my son's blanket near his chest. He gave me a deck of cards and went back to serve other passengers. In the next minutes, he'd check back on us numerous times. I remember concern about my son's ears and him feeling pain when the cabin de-pressurized. Biagio told me it might help to plan him suckling on a bottle at that time, much like adults' gum-chewing. Otherwise, the flight was a blur; a short haul arriving in Syracuse in less than 2 hours. His ears were fine.

To say I felt wholly broken is an understatement. Some people say, "When you're going through hell, don't stop." In retrospect, I'm certain that's how I got through the next 18 years' juggling of single-parenthood, careers (day job & evening consultancy business), evening adult education (mine), and family/household management without much support. All this with no local "village" of family members (since transferring to NC in 1983). I often felt I was on "automatic pilot". I didn't stop, I literally couldn't. Otherwise, I'm pretty sure my life would be far different today as a result.

Sharon Barrows Cooper

In retrospect, these were a few of the tools I used even prior to becoming a coach. I've later come to call them: DANDA, Pre-thinking, and Re-framing. I use these tools frequently in my coaching practice today, in numerous areas (Life, Business, Law of Attraction, Relationships, Recovery, Group, Weight Loss, etc.), with individuals, groups and companies.

DANDA was likely the first tool that was in motion as the marriage was teetering. DANDA is an acronym for what many believe are the 5 stages of grief or loss, as originally described by Kubler-Ross in her book "On Death & Dying", published in 1969. Just being familiar with these five stages of grieving or mourning is a tool that can help us navigate more clearly as we process our losses. These stages are also often shared in the recovery world. Denial, Anger, Negotiation (or bargaining), Depression (or sadness), and Acceptance. We don't do grief, it does us: and rarely straight from the first to the fifth, and poof we're golden. We traverse in and through, then back again a stage or two, and forward again, and back, over and over, until the loss is finally something we can wrap our minds, hearts, & spirit around... not one minute before we are "ready", getting us to a place of Acceptance. Denial, Anger, Negotiation/Bargaining, Depression/Sadness, Acceptance.

That cold day in 1979 was the day "the band aid of denial got ripped off" from my mindset of thinking that the marriage would get past the many differences we were realizing we had. No longer would I think "We'll figure it out. We'll live happily ever after just the way we once envisioned." We weren't seeking guidance or counsel; not from our wonderful parents, the clergy, a counsellor, not anyone. We were babies having just had a baby, and we seemingly, for the first time in my mind, didn't stand a chance together. The face of reality was far clearer than any time before in the previous two years of our emotional roller coaster of trying to figure things out. Our marriage was over, and I knew it. I somehow never felt the stage of Anger, although I know it must have been there in my deepest feelings somewhere. For me, the stages of Denial & Negotiating (we could make it if we just tried hard enough) for a couple of years, then Sadness for several months landed me into full-on Acceptance.

After 6 months of emotional healing in this safe & loving space with my parents, I was getting stronger & more like "myself" every day. This is the beginning point of a natural use of the "Pre-Thinking Tool" I now use in my coaching practice. One night over dinner Dad shared with me that I'd qualify for financial assistance, being an unemployed veteran & single Mom. Without hesitation, I shared I had a strong back and two good hands & felt I could figure it out for myself. Soon after, one day Dad came home, and instinctively, said it might be time to look for work, childcare, and an apartment. He'd seen a family friend who owned rental homes who after hearing my story, offered to rent a small apartment if I wanted to take a look at it. I did within a day or two.

In one week's fell swoop, I obtained employment, leased an apartment & moved in, and arranged excellent childcare for my son while I worked. I'd applied & interviewed for a job, received a job offer of minimum wage, negotiated it up to $4.85 per hour (the early 1980's), met with and felt peaceful about a childcare provider, and met with Bob B who approved me to lease the apartment 14 miles from where my parents lived, and 11 miles from the second college I'd attend evenings.

Sharon Barrows Cooper

The Pre-Thinking Tool is one of the tools that allows us to begin with the end in mind and accelerate reaching our milestones. We take the time to clearly identify and foresee the goal & desired results. We look at the needs, challenges, & possible roadblocks, as well as several other elements related to ourselves & the objective. In this way we set ourselves up for higher degrees of success as well as the most direct (think quickest) route to our desires. In about 7 days, I solved for "accelerated progress forward" childcare, employment, housing, and education… as well as proximity to family.

Thirdly, I used the tool I call "Re-Framing" in more situations than I could quantify in those next years as a single parent. Re-Framing is simply that; changing or re-framing the perceptions and the way I look at, see, and interpret the meaning of the various events and situations in my life. Instead of thinking, "I can't believe this is happening", "Why me?", or "This is horrible", I thought things that served me better like "What a Blessing to spend this special time as a new parent with my parents, new at Grand parenting", and "It's great to be able to show my son where I grew up and where part of him was rooted." Like the other tools, it was setting up my thinking in the most productive manner. I didn't change one fact; however, I greatly crafted the way I perceived & processed them.

So fast forward over 40 years. In 2005 after retiring as an SVP from a Fortune 100 Bank, I launched my career of passion in FT self-employment. I'm now running a thriving Life & Business coaching practice that serves many people & entities seeking various Custom Continuous Improvement solutions. Many coaches and leaders I now work with also once experienced difficult & challenging times. They too overcame tremendous odds, which resulted in their desire to not only help others do the same; but to help their clients take a more direct route to their own successes.

I'm grateful for my clients over the years, from whom I've learned a great deal. I'm currently in succession planning, seeking one qualified certified coach per state to mentor/train in my system; the one that includes the group blueprint I developed that grosses over $1000/hour for a 7-hour workshop serving over 75 people with no mailing list.

Are you ready to take your coaching practice/skills to the next level, or seek free information? If so, Barrows Cooper Coaching is accepting applications for our nationwide certified coaching network. For more information about Sharon, her company, and to claim your free consult and other free (no purchase required) items, contact her at: www.barrowscoopercoaching.com

BarrowsCooperCoaching.com

About Sharon Barrows Cooper

Sharon Barrows Cooper is the Founder and President of Barrows Cooper Coaching and Coach Plan Speak. She is a Continuous Improvement Expert with over 40 years of experience.

Upon retiring corporate America in 2005, Sharon launched her FT career of passion as a life/business coach.

She develops & facilitates custom programs, and is a motivational/keynote speaker. She delivers her services to individuals, groups, and companies. Sharon is a member of an international Master Mind serving clients across the globe. She also leads a charter community of like-minded individuals who serve and support.

Sharon is the author of the forthcoming "On Track Series"©, a unique continuous improvement work that focuses on success with sustainability. She's passionate about assisting individuals and organizations in obtaining remarkable clarity and resolve; thus achieving their goals & highest potential. Most importantly, Sharon provides personalized tools to her clients so they continue their successes long after the presentations and coaching sessions are completed. Sharon happily donates 50% of her revenue to 3 causes; Veterans & First Responders, Mental Health, & the Underserved.

Sharon Barrows Cooper

Through the Beginning: A Solstice Legacy

The highest and lowest points through the beginning of my life, personal transformation, and coaching career.

"Only you have to live in your own mind; make it a nice place to live."

by Glenn Deason

Transformation came to me when I least expected it. I was living a life of passion and fulfillment when disaster struck. My actions caused harm because I wasn't living intentionally. As a child, I had desires and chased them into my teens. In my twenties, those desires took hold of my life. I pursued them freely, but what seemed pleasurable wasn't always best for me or those around me.

Near the end of 2019, both the world and I began a transformative process. While the COVID pandemic shook society, I faced a metaphorical sickness in my heart and mind. I believed I was serving my purpose, but I was wrong. My life was being lived by a shadow of myself while I hid behind the eyes of a demon I created. The chaos in the world mirrored the chaos in my mind. I lost jobs, friends, vehicles, luxuries, and loved ones due to my negligent behavior. I found myself living in my mother's basement, unemployed, in therapy, battling addictions and my own mental fortitude. So, I wasn't exactly having a great time.

One night, during a depressive episode, I found myself atop a bridge, contemplating the traffic below. Debating whether to jump, I ultimately walked away, grateful for a second chance. My message to anyone in a similar situation: Seek emergency help. You are worth it. This world needs you.

After that, I realized I needed more help than I'd admitted. I found a phenomenal coach and an amazing therapist. Over the following year, I took an active role in improving my mental fitness. For me, training my body was always so much easier than training my mind. My therapist taught me how to interact with my body and emotions in a healthy way, while my coach taught me how to interact with life in a healthy way.

Since then, I've had many coaches, each with unique perspectives and insights. These are the most important things I have learned that will help you begin your own transformation:

Living with intention

Living with intention means making the conscious decision…to make a conscious decision. You get to choose the type of person you wish to be. Do you want to have a relaxed and aloof demeanor? Do you wish to take even trivial things seriously? Maybe a mix of the two? The power of choice lies with you.

We get to pick our regrets in life. And the decisions that we don't make consciously get made for us. Think about this the next time you get to make a decision.

Life has many paths for us to take. These decisions carry the weight of associated pain and pleasure, satisfaction and suffering. If you push to succeed in certain areas of your life, other areas may be sacrificed for the time being. You will find that if you seek to sacrifice as little as possible, you will find little satisfaction. And if you seek all of life's pleasures, you must bear the associated pain and sacrifice. Regardless of which path you choose; you have the power to accept that choice. If you can accept that choice when you are dealing with challenging times, and be grateful for the associated satisfaction, you will find solace in suffering.

Creating your ideal

My life changed the moment I realized I wasn't actively choosing who I wanted to be. The world is constantly vying for your time and attention. These are the most valuable and nonrenewable resources in your life. That's why companies want it, and your loved ones will notice its absence. Advertisers want you to see their thing. They want you to consume their content or product. If you don't choose what you want to see, the winner of the battle for your attention will choose for you. For me, I seek out media such as books and podcasts that cover the topics I'd like to be consuming. I create lists of things that I would like to contemplate so when I have time for rumination I can engage in a productive internal dialog. Once I envisioned what type of individual I would like to be, I was easily able to diagnose the habits that needed to be changed in my life and what to replace them with.

For those who struggle with creating an ideal to move towards, I recommend addition by subtraction, or process of elimination. Think of the things in your life that you aren't happy with. Select one and pick a replacement habit for that one thing. Most of us know what we do and don't like about ourselves, and the things we would like to change. Oftentimes, there is a simple yet difficult thing that we disregard while blaming some more complex or time-consuming issues.

If you struggle with identifying faults in your life, I recommend journaling. It's a way for us to communicate with our future selves. We often ask what advice we would give to our past selves, but rarely do we consider what we might want to remind our future selves. While this practice isn't an enjoyable one for everyone, in reviewing your own writing you will find common points over time. This is how I identified the biggest faults in my life. I have been journaling for two years and the issues I chastised myself for two years ago were the same from a year ago. Seeing this enabled me to realize that I had been blind to a massive piece of my self-improvement journey. My biggest faults would have remained hidden from me had I not put in the effort to write about them and review the writing over the required period of time.

The 3 Cs: Consume, Contemplate, Create

Consume: Think about what you consume in life. What information, media, and content are you allowing into your mind? What food, supplements, and substances do you allow into your body? And, most important, are these the things that you would like to consume? Are they serving your purpose? When you imagine the type of person you want to be, are these the things that person would consume? Once you start living with intention, and you know the direction you would like to be heading, eliminate from your life the things that are preventing you from achieving your goals.

Contemplate: This is somewhat affected by what you consume, so be cautious as to what you let into your mind. The act of processing information is just as important as consuming or creating it. There is an intrinsic power in the act of thinking. It is important to filter through all that you know in order to make your own belief system. In creating your own belief system, you define yourself, your reality, and in turn your life.

We must take care not to poison our thoughts with things that don't serve our purpose. For instance, try to not ruminate about negative things. Instead, focus on the things that make you happy, grateful, or motivated. If there is a situation or topic that is upsetting, be very methodical about how you approach it. If you think about why your day is so terrible all day long, there is no way for your mood to improve, even if your circumstances have. Ultimately, we want to consciously choose and have control over what our thoughts are going to be. Only you have to live in your own mind; make it a nice place to live.

Create: This C is the most nuanced and diverse because it encapsulates quite a wide variety of topics. It can refer to creating memories with loved ones, connections in your community, a family, a new business, a save file on a video game, art, or merchandise. Not to mention the habits we create which fundamentally change how we show up in the world. Think about the type of person you wish to become. What would that person create? Would they create healthy habits or self-destructive habits? If you want to be an artist, you need to create art. Whoever you wish to become, that is the person you need to create.

My Challenge for You Is to Ask Yourself:

"Am I living with intention?"

"Do I have an ideal to work towards?"

"Does what I consume, contemplate, and create align with that ideal?"

"What work, that I know I need to do, have I been avoiding?"

Then, get to it. After that? Do it again.

What made me decide to be a life coach?

There are people out there right now, living in a place that I have been in before. I can help them. It's as simple as that. I've now had a transformative experience to share with those who may feel like they are going through something alone when they don't need to be.

My first coach came to me at a crucial time in my life. Both my physical and mental fitness was the worst they had ever been. I will never forget the way my first coach made such a drastic impact with something as easy as a monthly phone call. This individual aided my journey, and in no small part, over a calendar year with a dozen phone calls. Yes, I had to do the work, take action, I don't mean to minimize the effort that takes. But twelve phone calls? It was at that moment that I had the realization of how much impact a great coach could have on a transformative process.

Since then, I've had many coaches to keep me on track. Each session brings clarity and direction, helping me map new territories of life. A coach serves as a guide through the changing world and makes the journey more navigable.

There are many wonderful coaches in this book. Find the ones who resonate with you and reach out. Remember, transformation is a continuous journey, and you have the power to shape your own path.

"Your life and actions are your Legacy. Your highest and lowest points; your Solstice." ~Glenn Deason

About Glenn Deason

Glenn Deason, CPC is a Certified Professional Coach and the founder of the coaching modality, Solstice Legacy. The mission of Solstice Legacy is to guide the development of individuals as they prepare for and navigate the highest and lowest points of their lives to produce the life they deserve.

Glenn has always been captivated by the hero's journey; the resolve to do good, the self-sacrifice for the sake of others, and overcoming insurmountable obstacles.

Driven by this passion, Glenn found himself involved in extreme sports and athletics from an early age. Finding his passion in the world of Parkour and performance arts, Glenn trained to be as capable as possible in any situation or environment.

He became "Coach Glenn" for the first time in the physical fitness world, as an acrobatics coach, training thousands of people to navigate and overcome physical obstacles for a decade.

Over time, Glenn realized he had so much more to offer. As a student of psychological and philosophical disciplines, Glenn has always been gathering the wisdom and knowledge that provide insights into life matters. Now, instead of just training people to navigate and overcome physical obstacles, Glenn is a Life Coach. He helps people navigate and overcome all types of obstacles in their life.

If you would like to follow what Glenn is working on or speak with him personally, please visit his website: www.GlennDeason.com.

Relationship Coaching is always about progress not perfection.

Truth is the foundation that opens the door to profound intimacy and deep connection. Let's find truth together.

"Finding the strength to look at who we truly are individually and sharing our authentic selves with another human is sometimes the only way forward in life. It sounds easy in theory but the work to deprogram and then reprogram is one of the hardest things we can ever do—and the only thing we MUST!"

by Jill Schwartz

A Relationship Coach is a strategic mediator, an emotional private investigator, and a personal guide to redirect you towards your correct path. We search for clues into the blueprint of your foundation, your attachment style, your love language, etc. It is in *this* understanding we see how to support your path.

Every detail of your life has already been ordained and delicately wired from birth. Then you begin your life as an adult. We present ourselves as fully formed individuals to the outside world, what we wear, where we live, what we drive, what we do for a living, etc. We rarely show our internal selves, who we are emotionally, spiritually, what our belief systems may be. Simply put, we have our own surface level idea of who we are, what we present, and what we like and don't like. If you are only capable of showing your external self, then that's the mirror you will attract. Share a deeper perspective and you will find like minds. You get what you give. Even when we are not in a romantic relationship, we are still in a relationship with ourselves. We are never alone. Try to always be mindful of that.

We have built our coping mechanisms and masks that we established to survive childhood, teenage years, and early adulthood. Then, we begin the journey of dating, relationships, and marriage. BAM, doors open and close quickly. We often find that connecting with a partner - regardless of sexual orientation – quickly becomes a complicated web of past and present ideations. It gets messy and sometimes unbearable. We can find ourselves stuck, confused, and lost. We become victims instead of victors.

My clients often don't know each other because they do not know themselves. They complain about finances, sex, and inability to resolve conflict–literally any conflict. They don't feel heard or seen or understood. They relentlessly face the price of not learning to communicate effectively. Much of what they have built over years was built on false information - fabricated within the fear of being vulnerable. They have been masking, pretending, and projecting doomed and inaccurate narratives. That's when they come to me, asking, "What's wrong with him/her?". I more often than not redirect the focus of blame: "What is wrong with YOU?"

As coaches we must be precise in our analysis - and have the ability to ask scrupulous, soul-bearing questions. Interpreting responses with clarity and create the absent trajectory. Now we're cooking with gas. Now we are on the road to liberation. What are our triggers, where did they originate from, how do we heal and evolve? Are we willing and capable? That part is up to each of us. My clients and myself.

I ask the mind-bending questions and my clients do the arduous work to grow with my guidance. We unveil what ails you when you allow me to introduce you to yourself. When we can accept and understand who we are, why and where we are, we can then share that information with our partner. It provides a wisdom and lucidity that bonds you as a couple and produces the most exquisite inner peace as all the broken pieces are swept away. You face your partner with naked emotion. You begin to see and hear each other in a new way. The old relationship is gone, and a new beautiful one begins creating a true authentic alignment. That's the long-term goal we should set to achieve. And IF, in the inevitability of discovery we reveal that people are best exiting a partnership, you move on with grace and courage, as to begin again with a more suitable match. Either way, everyone wins as progress is the goal.

My work as a coach requires me to be vulnerable with strangers. I sometimes share parts of my own life journey when it is necessary and appropriate. Sharing elements of my challenges and introduction to the beauty of truth, courage, and consistent change. I find it creates a profound connection with my clients - and the launch point for their own self-discovery. Everyone needs a safe person to share their story with, and the comfort of knowing that there is no judgment, only effort towards a course correction. Who are you, really? Don't be afraid, be excited! Be curious and make progress.

My approach is as simple as it is difficult to execute:

1.   What's your problem?

Couples individually tell me why they are unhappy with their relationship. This usually presents as the blame game. For example, "If He would just do X, then I wouldn't get triggered, so it's his fault and HE needs to change." and vice versa. I take the finger-pointing as the baseline of their own misunderstanding of what is actually happening. It is NOT entirely about what the other person is doing TO you, but what errors exist in YOUR programming. It is not that we are only ever the ones at fault. It is that we can only be responsible for how our own actions impact our relationships.

2.   Who Are YOU?

If you don't know the answer to that question, then that's where it begins. You must acknowledge who you are so you can express it to your partner. Time to remove your masks and really see yourselves and each other clearly. Hard work ahead. This is the process of SELF REALIZATION.

3.   Who are you TOGETHER?

What are each person's needs? What are each persons' desires? What are each persons' deal-breakers or non-negotiables? Do we want the same things? Are we aligned? Bottom line, ARE WE A MATCH?

4. How can we LEARN from our problems?

Mental Illnesses aside, find the cracks in the foundation and what can be learned. We work on communication, identifying triggers, emotional regulation, expectations, attachment styles, love languages, intimacy, sex, etc. Identify what can and cannot be resolved. MOVE TOWARDS ACCEPTANCE.

5. What TOOLS can we use?

I provide tools for success. Everyone requires specific tools based on the presenting issues. Every couple requires a unique approach. One size does not fit all. WISE MIND works wonders. Wise mind is the balance of rational logic with the sensitivity of emotion. The wise decision will come from the combination of intelligence and intuition which eliminates both overthinking and impulsivity.

6. Are we both WILLING and CAPABLE?

Make certain both partners are WILLING and CAPABLE. If this is not reciprocal, there is little anyone can do but head towards uncoupling. In such cases, FACE THE FEAR.

My ability to see what my clients cannot see is the core value I bring. I was born into a family of chaos and confusion. My parents were my programmers. That was both a blessing and a curse. And I am no different than anyone else. If I was a car, I would be a lemon. And as they say, if God gives you lemons, make lemonade. So, from a very young age, instead of playing outside with other children, I took on the task of staying inside my room (specifically inside my closet) and desperately tried to analyze what the hell was wrong with my parents. Why were they always fighting? Whose fault, was it? Who was right and who was wrong? Why can't they be nice to each other? Why am I sitting in my closet trying to figure them out? I was only ten years old.

On the outside we were the picture of perfection and success. Behind closed doors, we all hid. There was alcoholism, abuse, neglect, blame, anger, mental illnesses, outrageous fights. This was my blueprint. It set the stage for the future relationship dynamics that I both detested and engaged in. It's all I knew. It's what I was shown and taught.

But when I finally turned that ravenous curiosity, I had about my parents' issues back inward on myself, I began finding the solutions to unlearn all that had become so unhelpful. That set the stage to really begin helping other people. That's how my bitter past became such a sweet blessing, not only being able to personally relate to other peoples' trials and tribulations - but to be able to provide experientially proven techniques to help them disappear.

I have studied all forms of coaching modalities as well as psychology. I have turned what had become a side hustle into a lucrative business. I constantly put in more work to develop myself personally and professionally – it is my passion. More importantly, I now have such a sense of fulfillment, meaning, and purpose. My only regret is that I didn't discover WHO I WAS for so long. Better late than never it would seem.

To conclude, I leave all you expectedly complicated individuals and couples with this question:

Whilst you focus on what's wrong with your life and/or your partner, are you willing to explore, investigate, and own your own flaws? WHAT IS IT WORTH for you to discover if your lives and your relationships are aligned with who you are? And are they worth the challenge it takes to transform? What is that kind of power worth to you? Socrates said, "The unexamined life is not worth living." What is YOUR life worth, what is your truth worth? The answer is PRICELESS.

About Jill Schwartz

J_{ill} S_{chwartz} spent over 30 years in the Television Business in Game Shows, Award Shows, and Reality TV as a high-level Development and Acquisitions Executive. Biggest claim to fame is American Idol. Personal family tragedy forced her to reinvent at a late stage in life. Jill spent the last ten years growing her Life Coaching Career from a side hustle into a  thriving business. She studied the practices and methods of all the great leaders in this industry, Esther Perel, Tony Robbins, Mel Robbins, Jay Shetty, Hoffman, Gottman, MindValley, and more. Now she is a published author. Her background in Reality TV has turned into a career in REALITY period. Today is a chapter, tomorrow, the world. Jill is Professionally Certified in Solution Focused, Transformational, and Psychodynamic coaching approaches and a long-standing Member of the International Coaching Federation. For a free consultation you can connect with Jill through her website at http://JSLCON.com.

Your Kid's Life Coach

"It doesn't matter how young or old, what you tell yourself matters."

by Ingrid Dunham

I was always a dreamer and very literal. I remember going to Sunday School as a kid. One Sunday, the teacher told us we could move mountains if we believed we could. I reported back the next week that it actually didn't work because I stared at a mountain for a very long time, and it did not move an inch. I still laugh at myself over that.

Not much has really changed now that I am an adult. I still have a very strong faith and I am still very literal, but I do have a touch more common sense.

My Lessons, Wrapped Up as Gifts

My parents came to the United States in 1956 after WWII. My mother was pregnant with me at the time. My parents ended up going through a divorce a year later and I went back to Germany to live with my grandmother. She was like a mother to me and when my mother came back and once again brought me to the US when I was 7, I truly felt like my heart broke in two.

We came to the US and landed at LAX on a hot April night. My dad picked us up at the airport. We stayed with him until an argument broke out between him and my mother. My dad took off with me which was followed by court battles and a short stay in a foster home until dad got custody of me when I was 9.

My mother moved back to Germany, and I lived with my dad and my stepmom, who I came to love as my own mother.

My dad had a very kind heart and a really bad temper. He was tormented by what I think must have been PTSD. He wasn't the only one who had a hard time, unfortunately, that all flowed downhill. Sometimes at a trickle and sometimes like a flood.

When I was 9, we moved to a little town by the ocean. I made great friends. We would be gone all day during the summer, catching frogs, fishing and just having fun.

Having a rough home life just seemed like part of the life package. I remember thinking that everyone had something that was hard that they had to deal with. My two besties I hung out with had their own stories. One of them had a dad who was an alcoholic, and the other one had a mom who left their dad for the school principal.

We moved again when I was 13. I would have given my right arm at the time to stay where I was. Things went downhill and at 17 I ran away from home. I thought that was my solution at the time to becoming an adult and making my own decisions. I ended up with 3 days at Juvenile Hall. I landed there because my dad had overreacted, and I had a choice to go to Juvenile Hall or go home. The 3rd day I finally agreed to speak to my parents. My dad wanted to take me to Germany. I remember thinking," You don't just get to return me". I decided to go

Ingrid Dunham

with the guarantee of a roundtrip ticket. I was able to see my grandmother again after 10 years. It would be the last time I got to hug that sweet woman. Sometimes gifts come wrapped in funny packages.

I came into adulthood carrying a really good toolbox. I always believed God had my back and that everything would be ok. I felt grateful for my lessons and came away with a realization that we all do the best we can with what we have at the time. Everyone has their own struggles to fight through.

Somehow, I knew what life should be like and what it could be like. I want people to know it can be better, life doesn't have to be so hard. Not to minimize what people are going through, but just to let them know that it is possible to swing that pendulum the other way. It is possible to smile more and look at things a little differently.

It's at the core of what I have always known to be true and everything that I have learned has supported that. I have always been so excited by the idea that I could help make someone else's life a little better. I believe there is always a solution to every problem. Sometimes the solution is we have to think about it in a different way. There is so much power in that.

In 2009 I became a certified life coach with Wainwright Global. We had an assignment that had such a huge impact on me and my coaching practice. We were asked to partner with a classmate and take turns asking what they wanted their life to look like. Then, we wrote their story for them so they could actually feel that as if their life was just as they imagined. It was so powerful and the catalyst for so many stories I have written for adults and children.

That same year I became a certified hypnotist. I learned more about how our subconscious mind works and how it is our hard drive. Our experiences and our thoughts and feelings about those experiences get stored in that hard drive. The good news is we can change that hard drive by writing a new story. Our mind truly believes what we tell it.

I have helped kids get over fears, have better study habits, go through life with more confidence, stop sucking their thumb, and wetting the bed, all by writing a story and allowing their minds to visualize themselves being successful. I have learned if we show our mind what we want, it works on finding a way to make that happen. It amazes me every day.

It doesn't matter how young or old, what you tell yourself matters. I work with adults as well. Do you have something in your life that you feel would make you happier if you could just change it?

About Ingrid Dunham

Ingrid Dunham is a Certified
Professional Coach and
Certified Hypnotist. Ingrid is
known for helping children and
adults find a little more
happiness through writing
personalized positive
visualization stories.

She started her journey as
"Dear Fran" in grade school
and has loved helping people
find solutions ever since.

She lives in Maine with her husband and loves spending
time with her kids and grandkids.

She has a passion for helping people see that life does not
have to be so hard and that there is always a solution. You
can reach Ingrid at www.yourkidslifecoach.com. She
would love to hear from you.

Coaching Helped to Unleash My Greatness:

You TOO Can Transform from Good to Great

"We All Have Greatness Inside of Us Begging for Release!"

by Lesia L. Crumpton-Young, PhD., MBA

My journey to realizing the power of coaching began when I found my mother crying profusely and saying that she wanted the best life for herself, and her children, and she was fearful that it would be impossible because she was newly divorced. My journey continued as I encountered other clients crying, depressed, anxiety-ridden, unhappy, overweight, experiencing career suicide, having family concerns, financial worries, self-doubt, and other paralyzing problems. I have always felt compelled to help enhance the lives of others and to do whatever I could to ensure they were achieving their greatest potential and living their best life.

I was innately drawn to doing whatever was needed to make sure that my mother 's dream of us having a fabulous life as well as the dreams of my other clients come to fruition. As a result, I became a very strategic, hard-working and resourceful person with a positive and optimistic outlook. I learned the importance of seeking the advice and assistance of others and I found myself not allowing fear, doubt, or worry to keep me from being successful. I also found myself not allowing the limiting thoughts of others to bridle my excitement and enthusiasm, nor curtail the endeavors that I embarked upon. I also found myself constantly dreaming, always having a big thought or bright idea. As a result, I worked to push myself beyond my comfort zone and beyond what I thought I was capable of, and it was always amazing to find out that I was capable of so much more than ever imagined. My journey of battling to become one of the first African American females to earn a PhD in engineering, the quest to accomplish the impossible dream of becoming one of the first African American females in the country to become a full professor in engineering. As a result, I quickly progressed professionally and won the Trailblazer Award, the Women in Science and Technology Award, the Stem Innovators' Award, the black engineer of the Year award, and the US Presidential Award for excellence in science, engineering, and mathematics mentoring. At that moment, I realized not only had I overcome my struggles and achieved many goals, but receiving this award meant that I had done an outstanding job of mentoring and helping others achieve their wildest dreams.

After embracing this realization, I was on fire because I was convinced that I could parlay my mentoring skills to become an outstanding coach for others. I firmly believed that my trials, tribulations, and triumphs could be valuable lessons that could help me assist others. Thus, I reaffirmed my compulsion to enhance the lives of others by coaching them to achieve their desired goals and priorities.

As a result, I began my coaching efforts. I acquired certificates in both life coaching and career coaching. In working with clients, I specialize in the synergy of helping individuals enhance their life by enhancing their careers. Additionally, throughout my coaching career, I have helped clients overcome many of these issues and more. Even if they were stifled by family problems, financial problems, career concerns, professional pursuits, weight issues, untapped potential, pessimistic thoughts, naysayer mentality, or limiting views influenced by fear, doubt, worry, or other concerns, I have been successful in coaching them to resolve the issues.

I'm a person that believes that great things happen in your life when you make sure that great things happen in the lives of others. I firmly believe that it is the responsibility of a great coach to enlighten their clients, elevate their clients, and most importantly empower them so they believe that they can accomplish their wildest dreams and transform their lives.

Throughout my career, I have been blessed to coach many individuals. Some Testimonials from my Coaching Clients when asked to describe "The best aspects of their coaching sessions" include:

Making the connection between my roles/responsibilities and goals and then linking all of that with my daily schedule/time distribution. Having the "light go on" in my head about being intentional with strategy and time management.

The time to focus on what I feel that I need to do to be more effective. Dr. Young's ability to reframe issues that I am thinking of in a way that doesn't diminish their importance and increases hope for making realistic changes for improvement. Her willingness to be open about relevant issues also was comforting and encouraging.

Being coached by talking through what it is I want to accomplish by simply answering questions and having action items form in my head as I'm "talking out loud". Even though the session centered on me answering questions, I still received good feedback or additional questions that were helpful in "painting a picture" of where I want to be.

Seeing an exponential increase in my research productivity due to the coaching received. Also, starting to see the roadmap for the next few years of my career take form and line up in a very strategic manner.

Seeing the vision/direction for my future take shape during the discussions of our session (with action items that are always effective, practical, and achievable). Seeing my goals being accomplished and my research productivity skyrocket. Waking up excited about my day, instead of dreading it because of everything I need to do (not waking up feeling overwhelmed).

Resolution:

Through the power of coaching, I have been extremely successful in helping so many individuals ascend to positions of leadership in the fields of engineering, science, technology, mathematics, business and finance, sales, education, agriculture, health sciences, psychology, communications, fundraising, philanthropy, entrepreneurship, and higher education. I've actively helped to propel their careers to the ranks of presidents of institutions and executive leaders of various organizations within our nation. My personal journey of advancement is a major component of why I'm successful, and my educational background in industrial engineering where I learned the importance of utilizing tools and techniques that help organizations be successful contributed to the effectiveness of my coaching programs. I learned to use proven tools and techniques for organizations and customize them to help individuals achieve success. I published the book entitled "Key Productivity and Performance Strategies to Advance Your Career." This book discusses 10 strategies that can be used to enhance your career trajectory. For example, while coaching, I've helped individuals set clear goals and utilize strategies to accomplish their goals, assisting them in employing decisive decision-making strategies, pushing them to adopt the get things done mentality, encouraging them to abandon thoughts of fear, doubt and worry, lead them to overcome the limiting views in their minds and silence their inner critic, and enlightened them on the importance of chasing the fat rabbits in life. Additionally, I've also worked with clients on the importance of concentrating on closing and completing their goals in life because the power of focus is critical to accomplishing your dreams and aspirations. Also, I help my clients establish a paradigm for consistency. I've taught them the art of efficiently allocating their resources, and I've also helped them to determine the importance of persistence as well as the criticality of proceeding boldly and courageously when pursuing goals and ambitions in life.

Realization:

As I reflect upon my coaching journey, I am the coach that believes that everyone was designed for greatness, and I am the coach that helps individuals unleash their greatness! I am the coach that encourages individuals when they are ready to be great. I look forward to continuing to work as a Coach that transforms the lives of others. When Coaching, I utilize specific strategies and initiatives and I'm very intentional in creating customized coaching services, so my clients do achieve success! We don't just talk about it. We don't just dream about it. We develop a plan. We create implementation strategies to employ. We motivate and inspire ourselves to execute those strategies, so their desires come to fruition.

A Critical Coaching Question For YOU:

What are you willing to do today that will help to Unleash Your Greatness Within?

About Lesia L. Crumpton-Young, PhD., MBA

Dr. Lesia Crumpton Young is the recipient of the US Presidential Award for Excellence in Mentoring, and she is an accomplished Certified Life and Career Coach. She is regarded for transforming the lives of her clients by helping them achieve their greatest desires. She authored the "You've Got the Power  workbook series!" and the book entitled "Key Productivity and Performance Strategies to Advance Your Career". She is presently the host of the Heart 2 Heart with Dr. CY Radio show and Podcast where she engages her clients and others in essential conversations necessary to transform their lives. She's committed to implementing strategies and techniques to ensure her clients achieve their highest potential and unlock their greatness! She completed a bachelor's, master's, and a PhD in Engineering and an MBA. She has 25 years of experience in executive leadership, she held the position of President at Texas Southern University, and she currently serves as President and CEO of the Greatness Gurus Corporation.

I am the Coach focused on helping others unleash their greatness! if you are ready to unleash your greatness quickly go to my website www.greatnessgurus.com to join the greatness community and register to win a free gift of Coaching that is guaranteed to transform your life and help you achieve your greatest desires. I look forward to working with you to unleash your greatness. Also, connect with me on all our social media channels @Drcrumptonyoung and @Greatnessgurus.

Lesia L. Crumpton-Young, PhD., MBA

The Spirit of Coaching

"After that fateful night I woke up, "clothed, and in my right mind." - Luke 8:35"

by Jacqueline Piña

Would you like to hear one of the shortest ghost stories of all time? It's a little gem I used to inspire my students in creative writing class. It's an old British folk tale and it goes like this: "He woke up frightened and reached for the matches; and the matches were put in his hand." Just a few words can tell quite a story. We don't really need to know what happened before or after to be captured or entertained by the story. Similarly, we only need a snippet of someone's life events to understand the big picture. But to gain valuable lessons we can dig a little deeper and find something called the rest of the story. Here's mine.

You may have heard it said there's no such thing as overnight success. But what do you think about overnight healing? Well, that's what happened to me at a picturesque place called Redondo Beach in March of 2009. I was in love and living in a beautiful cottage by the sea. I also had my dream job, and everything seemed to be quite good. But not really.

Behind closed doors I was deep in spiritual battle and turmoil, fighting to slay my inner demons. Although I was living in such an idyllic place with love and support all around me, things were not right in my spirit. I was not healthy. I didn't fully understand it at the time, but I suffered greatly from the effects of historical trauma and unresolved childhood grief. Instinctively I moved to the beach to heal. In essence, and out of sheer desperation, I was already doing the work and praying a lot.

And then tragedy struck. My precious Yorkshire Terrier, Gigolo, was hit by a car and didn't make it. It was a devastating loss. He was my baby boy and my best friend. I called him Jiggy, and he was as spunky, smart and loving as any puppy could be. He grew to be seven pounds of pure love. On that sad night I made a bed for Jiggy for the last time as I put him in a wicker basket on the porch. Saying goodnight to my boy, I asked him one final question, "Who's going to take care of me now?" I blessed him and thanked him and went inside.

I don't know how I was able to sleep that night, but I did. I woke up early and made plans for later that afternoon to bury Jiggy at another location. I was heartbroken but carried on with things at home until it was time to go. By noon I was plagued with a feeling other than sadness. It was that nagging feeling of forgetting something. I tried to think of what it was I was "forgetting." I even looked over my to-do list and calendar. What was I missing? It was like something inside of me was trying to draw my attention. The feeling was becoming annoying, and I just wanted to get back to my current misery.

Then I wondered why I wasn't drinking yet. That was it! Suddenly a warmth came over me from head to toe as I realized I was "forgetting" to drink. It was early afternoon and normally I would be struggling; praying for strength, begging myself, wracked with guilt and shame. I'd be trying to figure out why I was unable to stop reaching for that bottle of vodka. At that point I had tried everything but in-patient treatment. The drinking only got worse. I was waiting for a break in my work schedule to sneak into rehab. Meanwhile, all I could do was pray, even as the alcohol was going down my throat, still I prayed.

My faith in Creator never wavered. I prayed for strength, for release. I read every self-help book and watched every spiritual program I could find. I was in despair. I simultaneously felt that I was going to die very soon, or a true miracle was going to happen. Change was coming.

That day in 2009, all the desperation, craving, desire, need, focus, and overall spirit of addiction had vanished. Just gone. After that fateful night I woke up, clothed and in my right mind. Like the story in Luke describing the man out of whom devils had departed. Totally healed. Release had happened.

You see, on the night I lost Jiggy I surrendered past and present pain. I knew I couldn't do it without him. So, I let go of it. I thought of how this strong little dog was always there for me. Especially a few years before when I'd find myself on the sofa, alone in the dark. It would be late afternoon when I'd started sitting there, cuddled with the phone and a big glass of wine. By sunset, I'd be well on my way, beyond buzzed. I was too busy drinking and chatting to turn the lights on, and it would be a shock at the end of that last call. The seemingly sudden darkness would envelop me like a cold blanket. I found my center by looking out of the window at the streetlamp. Self-pity would take over and I'd begin to cry.

That's when my seven-pound angel would appear. Jiggy would jump onto my stomach and walk up my chest to my face. He would patiently wait to make eye contact as I sobbed, swaying my face back and forth. As he caught my eye in the moonlight, he would lovingly begin to kiss the tears off my cheeks. I would take immediate comfort and quickly get myself to bed. That's what I meant when I asked who would care for me after Jiggy left. Maybe that's when the miracle happened. Something shifted.

Now you might have a different theory, but this is mine. Maybe Jiggy heard me in Heaven and asked Creator to give me extra blessing in his absence? That's it, love. Miracles happen in the realm of love, right? From that night forward I have not craved a drop of alcohol. I believe I was healed as I slept.

My medical doctor was astonished at my next visit. On this day my lab work and exams showed healthy liver and kidney function, and my blood sugar numbers were excellent. I was told that at my level of chemical dependence I would have experienced delirium tremens, or life-threatening withdrawal. Although my healing miracle happened overnight, the rest of my story happens over a lifetime. The funny thing is everyone happily gathers for a good ghost story but start sharing a miracle story and the room clears out quickly! Whichever way we look at it, it's all supernatural. And supernatural is cool, am I right?

It's now summer of 2024, and I live in a dream castle in a five-acre forest. I just passed my 15-year wellness anniversary, and I'm celebrating life by enjoying the view and walking the path of peace with inner joy. I live to encourage others to seek healing with all their hearts. It's

Jacqueline Piña

such a deeply personal journey for each individual but we all meet at the crossroads of spirit and truth, healing and hope. We are not alone at heart.

This brings us to my brand of coaching. I coach the spirit of a person. I'm a spiritual coach. Different than a personal cheerleader or counselor, I teach spiritual lessons and design curriculum that meets the specific needs of an individual or organization. As a certified professional life coach my work is rooted in cognitive behavioral therapy, but as a teacher I integrate the needs of the spirit for my clients: Body, Mind, Spirit. Two out of three ain't bad, as they say. I really don't see myself as your P.E. teacher any time soon. But I do enjoy the heck out of helping you heal things in your beautiful mind and teaching you how to anchor into your true spirit. It might sound all woo-woo, but it's about learning how to quiet repetitive thoughts and seeking your most authentic self. The spiritual aspect of my coaching has nothing to do with religion, dogma, or a specific belief system. It's about the whole person, minus the physical marathon training. But never say never.

As for life outside of professional coaching, I am blessed and busy with beautiful grandkids and a wonderful husband as we are starting a mini farm! We look forward to sharing our new homesteading adventures with you. Also, after working with the unhoused and women's groups for over a decade, I'm creating a broader community-based nonprofit that provides educational/spiritual support. Please join us via the links below and keep us in your prayers. "May the God of hope fill you with all joy and peace in believing so that by the power of the Holy Spirit you may abound in hope." Romans 15:13

My personal spiritual journey has been one of building bridges, a change from blowing them up, to God be the glory. My Apsáalooke/Crow tribal name is Sacred Tobacco Woman. It was a big name given to a little girl. It's taken silver streaks in my hair to realize what standing in that name means: Bridging that which is earthly to that which is sacred. You are sacred.

Inspirational articles

https://www.bellaonline.com/archive/nativeamerican

Free strategy consultation

https://sacredtobaccowoman.com

Join our email lists sacredtobaccowoman@gmail.com

About Jacqueline Piña

Jacqueline Piña, M.A. Ed.,
CPC, is a proud Crow Tribal
member. As a child Jacqueline
was named Sacred Tobacco
Woman. It was Jacqueline's
beloved grandmother who
taught her the wisdom and
power of faith and love.

Jacqueline moves through the
world inspired by her heritage
and trust in Creator. Jacqueline
helps those suffering from the effects of transgenerational
trauma. As an active path seeker her passion is to explore
the realms of faith and spiritual practice to transform lives.

A dedicated humanitarian and life-long learner, her heart
for service began in her youth. Presently, Jacqueline serves
as founder and executive director of One Heart Sacred
Alliance, a nonprofit providing educational services.

As a street pastor and spiritual life coach Jacqueline has
been entrusted with many sacred stories. She dedicates her
life to speak light over the power of fear.

Jacqueline served as Editor for the Native American site at
BellaOnline.com, publishing articles on historical trauma
and finding peace through Native Wisdom.

Central Washington University B.A. Ed. (K-8), magna
cum laude Lesley University M.A. Ed. Curriculum Design

and Development, Wainwright Global, Inc. Professional Life Coach Certification CPC, Universal Life Church Ordination

In 2009, Jacqueline experienced intense spontaneous healing from her addiction resulting from unresolved childhood grief.

Sacredtobaccowoman@gmail.com

Mastering the Craft: The Ability to Coach is an Acquired Talent

"Coaching is not just about assisting others' growth, knowledge, and skills, but a mindset and way of life."

by Carolyn E. Scott

I have learned that great business coaching stems from Experience-Based Learning. In my field of work as a Human Resources professional my area of specialty is in Organization Development. I consider my ability to practice executive, professional business coaching each day to be a bonus. As I engage with my professional network of coaches in various industries, we each recognize that our coaching style is as unique as our individual fingerprint. My coaching style is a direct biproduct of my diverse real-world experience. I have immense respect and appreciation for the opportunities that I have in my field to collaborate with individuals from varied backgrounds, and the exposure I gain to differing viewpoints and problem-solving approaches. This level of diversity enriches my understanding of the challenges and opportunities that business leaders face, enabling me to offer adaptive, customized, effective business coaching. I also understand and appreciate that coaching in any area of discipline requires a commitment, a commitment to continuous learning. My ability to also practice as a business coach in my field of work as an executive level Human Resources professional demonstrates my strong commitment to helping others to reach their potential and achieve their desired goals.

Over fifteen years as a business coach, throughout my career, I have found that I also benefit through my ability to build lasting, strong, trusting relationships. This in turn has served to enrich and grow my personal and professional network. As an organization business coach, my ability to contribute and to help set the bar for increased standards for business excellence holds significant importance to me, the individuals I serve and their respective organizations. I see firsthand how coaching business leaders creates a direct return benefit to their organization's work culture and bottom line. Leaders who engage in business coaching can uncover untapped competitive gains through several key mechanisms:

1) Enhanced strategic clarity
2) Focused leadership development
3) The ability for business leaders to identify and address their weaknesses and strengths
4) Boost innovation within their business by challenging the status quo and stimulating creative thinking
5) Improve efficiency and productivity through deployment of process optimization and engaging performance enhancing strategies
6) Informed decision making and cultivating a growth mindset. Better decisions can position a business to capitalize on market opportunities and to respond more agilely to changes.

Business coaching fosters an environment where strategic clarity, effective leadership, operational efficiency, and innovative thinking converge, leading to significant competitive advantages.

An organizational business coach should have a blend of skills, qualities and a deep understanding of business dynamics and organization development to also include:

1) A strong business acumen - an ability to understand various aspects of business to include marketing, finance and operations;
2) The ability to analyze business models specific to organization design and organization development;
3) Use of analytical thinking to help others to systemically dissect problems; and last
4) Emotional Intelligence which enables one's ability to coach while recognizing and managing emotions in themselves and others.

Emotional intelligence is a core skill that builds trust and rapport, enhances communications through effective listening and enables one's ability to read non-verbal cues, it also helps with conflict resolution and the ability to work through emotional challenges that are often present even in organization business coaching. Fostering emotional intelligence helps business leaders to develop crucial leadership and people skills. These skills are essential for their design and containment of long-term personal and professional success. As a business coach, my success in this discipline is highly contingent upon my ability to demonstrate credibility, trustworthiness, and the ability to act with unshakable ethics and integrity. Each of these skills as defined herein contributes to my ability to facilitate an authentic, integrated approach to coaching.

As an organizational business coach, I have personally witnessed how an effective and sound delivery of executive coaching leads to helping leaders to learn to embrace challenges that persist in the face of setbacks and to see effort as a path to mastery. My goal as a business coach is to help others to carve a path to achieve their full potential and long-term success. This involves collaborating with leaders to help each to provide added clarity to their vision and goals for both the short-term and long term. To help each to create a clear action plan to enhance their individual and unique leadership skills, and for each to achieve personal and sustainable growth. As a business coach, I aim to empower others to make informed decisions, inspire "initiative-taking leadership," to seize the moment and to realize meaningful success.

Organizational coaching is an in-depth, multifaceted process, squarely centered on our ability as coaching professionals to use our talent and experience to develop and influence future leaders. Organizational coaching provides rich, rewarding life-changing experiences, both for the coach and those that we serve.

"Coaching is the universal language of change and learning." — CNN.

Organizational coaching is my passion and personal calling, and there is nothing more rewarding.

Carolyn E. Scott

About Carolyn E. Scott

Carolyn E. Scott, Thought Leader, Change Agent - is an experienced organizational business coach known for her expertise in helping businesses and leaders achieve their goals. Carolyn attributes her background of ten years in operations management in an executive capacity throughout her career with honing her skills in the discipline of organization  dynamics, coaching, training and leadership development. Carolyns focus is to work with leaders to enable their ability to create efficient organizational structures, enhance team performance and to foster a growth-oriented culture. Her coaching methods include: Strategic Planning, helping businesses to identify their vision, set achievable goals and develop action plans to reach those objectives; Leadership Development, training leaders to be effective, inspirational, and strategic in their roles to include one-on-one coaching, workshops and seminars; Team Building, enhancing team dynamics and communication to improve collaboration and productivity; Change Management, guiding organizations through periods of transition, such as mergers and restructuring. Carolyn's approach is highly personalized, recognizing that each organization has its own distinct and unique challenges and opportunities. She uses a combination of analytical tools, proven methodologies and her extensive experience in staff and operations and organization management to provide tailored solutions.

You can find Carolyn E. Scott, M.A., Chief of Staff, Human Resources Professional and Executive Coach on LinkedIn here:

https://www.linkedin.com/in/carolyn-e-scott-m-a-phr-bcc-shrm-cp-0b050a7/

Born to Coach

"How I found my Life Mission"

by Ginger Purewal

Is it possible that even as a child I was already practicing coaching skills? In a large family there is always one that stands out as the "wise one", and that was my mother,

There are many traits I got from my mother. At an early age I watched her advise her closest friends and family on how to navigate life's challenges. I learned what it takes to be a good listener and when to provide support and when to simply be present. I wanted to be helpful too, like my mother. My motto quickly became, "How can I help?"

As an adult I grew these skills unknowingly and my natural charismatic personality attracted many friends and family.

However, deep down in my soul, I lacked something that was the key to my future; my confidence and my own self-worth.

Why is it so easy to help everyone else with their problems and yet so difficult to solve your own? I'm the one who needed answers, healing. So, my inner journey began!

In 2010, I came across the Fowler Wainwright International Institute of Professional Coaching Course and signed up for it.

That was one of the best decisions I ever made. This program was exactly what I needed to help me get out of myself and follow my passion of helping others all while helping myself.

At the time, I already had a certification as a Certified Massage Practitioner, and I was ready to open my own practice and blend both Massage and Coaching depending on the client's needs.

A deep massage softens the heart and helps people release emotional issues that may have been hidden deep in the subconscious for years. With my counseling skills, I was ready to support them in their healing process. What a rewarding feeling it was to help my clients in this way!

Although I was successful, I knew I needed to do more, and that my true mission was about to unfold.

In August of 2022, my contract as a Financial Counselor at the local hospital ended and was decided not to renew, therefore I was a free agent and decided to take the remaining year off.

In the meantime, I had an intimate conversation with the Universe that I wasn't going to apply for any jobs and to just send me to my next assignment.

In November 2022 I was driving to my daughter's home for Thanksgiving and received a telephone call from the owner of Freedom Home Health-Hospice.

She asked what I was doing and I replied "enjoying life".

She then asked if I was working and perhaps interested in meeting with her. I replied, "I will contact you after the holidays."

In 2023, I was hired as a Bereavement Coordinator, to provide grief support to family members, whose loved ones passed away. I realized very quickly that in this field, I would be using the most sensitive coaching skills in my tool box.

In a state of grief, a loved one is very vulnerable and feels that no one could possibly understand their pain. When one is in such distress you need to get yourself out of the way and create a comforting loving and sacred space for them to heal and meet them exactly where they are.

I have truly found my life mission in the coaching field. I use my counseling skills daily in the most intimate way.

After the death of a loved one, I continue the counseling sessions for one year and many of them have expressed how easy it has been talking with me.

I have developed deep relationships with many who have been open and receptive to receiving guidance of how and where to begin living their lives without their loved ones.

I have a long list of testimonials that attest to having truly mastered my life's mission as a coach and that is a very rewarding feeling.

Here are some heartwarming testimonials I would like to share;

"My experience with Ginger is always positive. She has a generous and calming nature. She doesn't let life's difficulties to get her down and shares that optimism with others. She always has a smile and gives her full attention to everyone she meets." ~ Sumiko

"Ginger is a beautiful person inside and out. You will be inspired by her and uplifted by her gentle manner, kindness, her patience and her deep wisdom. She will be an enriching resource for all of her clients and I highly recommend her." ~ Terri

"Ginger has a gift of soulfully helping people to connect with their whole self, to their untapped potential and bring into realization and congruence their abilities, interests, thoughts and actions." ~ Aman

"From the beginning, I innately trusted Ginger for her wisdom, authenticity, kind, nonjudgmental, and personal and spiritual awareness. Ginger's very presence is healing, she listens to the words I don't say and in her uncanny way, always inspires me toward balance in my life. Her experience and knowledge are unending resources for anyone who is lucky to know her." ~ Diana

"The room lights up with her energy when she enters. Ginger captivates you with her infectious smile and positive vibes. Her voice is calming, comforting, sensitive, and supporting. She wills you to a place of center and balance where you feel encouraged, nourished, and loved. That is what it's like to come into her sphere; every time I see her." ~ Dilpreet

"As a physician and nephrologist, who sees patients who are often times exasperated with their medical problems it is refreshing to see someone, who understands not only their medical needs, but their emotional and spiritual needs as well. Ginger is that individual, who is able to provide this type of support. It really does not matter if your needs are only emotional or spiritual; a conversation with Ginger is the remedy you deserve." ~ Dr. Fraser

"Ginger has always had a significant impact on how I live my life. She offers a unique calm approach to setting boundaries and helping me to make the right decisions for my life. She offers inner strength that is contagious. Getting to work with her is a true privilege." ~ Aherne

"I feel so blessed to have known Ginger for about 10 years now. I feel like everyone who knows her, cherishes their conversations and time with her. I was in my mid 20's when we started working together as fellow body workers and she was such a positive influence on me. I am genuinely excited to see what she has in store to help her clients flourish as much she has in life!" ~ Tawney

"It has been my pleasure to know Ginger for over a decade. My experience with her is that she consistently approaches life with a positive attitude and a smile on her face. Even in challenging times in her life, she has remained optimistic. She learns from her experiences, and then shares her wisdom with others. She is an excellent listener and gives her full attention to all of those she meets. I highly recommend her!" ~ Carolyn

About Ginger Purewal

Ginger Purewal is a seasoned professional coach with over 14 years of experience in coaching. She is a Bereavement Coordinator for Freedom Home Health/Hospice

She uses her gift of intuition and compassion to help guide others to brighter days. Somehow knowing just what to say. Her eagerness and positivity are inspiring and contagious.

With a calm and positive nature, she uses her unique blend of guidance and support for one's own journey of self-discovery. This contributes to long lasting happiness and the growth that comes with self-love.

Conversations with Ginger - Contact: (530) 682-6499

Coaching For Success

Building your future on the past foundation.

"Everyone brings skills to the game and great coaches understand how to draw those skills out and achieve the "W.""

by Dr. Mae Killebrew-Mosley

As a child growing up in rural Mississippi in the 60s and 70s, I would lay on my porch on hot summer days and dream about what the future held for me. I knew there was more in life for me beyond the three-mile drive from our farm to the town of Lambert. I was number seven in the house of nine siblings and two loving parents, Mr. Floyd and Mrs. Earnestine. Life was simple, and their ability to navigate finances, farming, and parenting was masterful. They had one simple goal for themselves; raise their children to be successful. Defining exactly what success meant and how it would be accomplished was to be revealed over time and not in the moment.

Now, as a professional career coach, I reflect back on how my parents masterfully used all of the techniques that defines a Master Coach. They developed Master Coaching skills due to situations and circumstances. They had great listening skills by sorting through the noise to hear each child. Active listening is a valuable trait for coaches to have. They had compassion, which is another valuable trait of great coaches. They had a genuine interest in the successful outcome for all children. They assessed the skills and abilities of each one and developed a plan to win. Sometimes we didn't agree with our parents and wanted to pursue our own ambitions and dreams. When disagreements occurred, as great coaches, they understand how to redirect the conversation to achieve the "W" (win). Their task was to translate insights into meaningful actions to support attaining our goals.

Everyone brings skills to the game and great coaches understand how to draw those skills out and achieve the "W." There is no one size fits all and therefore influencing the outcome of lives across nine children was a major challenge. We had different likes and dislikes. Each of us possessed different talents and skills. Our personal stories were different and so were our personalities and aspirations. Motivation is one of the most challenging steps in coaching. What drives one person may have no effect on another. Obviously, spreading time across nine children to understand how to motivate them would require a major undertaking and a tremendous amount of time. They had experience at how to motivate them to prepare for the "W." The key is not the 'will to win'… everybody has that. It is the will to prepare to win that is important," Bob Knight.

The key to developing the will to win is understanding what holds one back. Asking the right questions and identifying their aspirations, hopes and goals for the future is essential for developing the plan to move forward. Mr. Floyd and Mrs. Earnestine observed, instructed and advised each child along the way as their stories unfolded.

They identified three goals they believed were core to success and getting to the "W." Their approach was for the nine children to have the same three goals. First, get an education. They clearly understood the route to success required knowledge and education. Education helps us understand and make sense of the world around which leads to better decision making. Second, be honest and an upright citizen. They knew that having integrity was important as you move through life and engage with others. Establishing yourself as a person with integrity and willing to stand for what is right for human kind is crucial to contributing to a better society. Finally, the third goal was, whatever you do, do your best to be the best. By always doing your best, positions you for success. This allows you to identify and act on variables you can control that influences the outcomes. This inspires you to create conditions to prepare for the "W.".

When roadblocks and setbacks arose, my parents could offer encouragement and redirect the course of action based on the challenge. They understood the personal fears, challenges and oppositions to the route for success. Obstacles and barriers due to race, gender, finance, background and the many other factors that play a role in how you show up must be addressed. Growing more dissatisfied with the systems that interfere, interrupt and even prevent success, forced me to redirect my attention to find the "W" multiple times in my life. When my professional career is not landing the position, title, or finances desired, then where should I look to find the "W." There were times when I knew I was the most qualified and yet, I was not selected for the position. I was disappointed and often felt that I had the education, I certainly had integrity, I had done my best to be the best. Why was there no "W?"

Over time, I decided that I would apply the simple approach that Mr. Floyd and Mrs. Earnestine encouraged and promoted in my early childhood years. One or more disappointment does not mean the game is over. Each time, I have dusted myself off, licked my wounded spirit and moved on. I pursued more education. I have enough training certifications to plaster all of the walls in the White House, and yet, I have been denied positions I knew I had more on paper than the others who participated in the interviews. Why was there no "W?" I firmly believed I had done my best to be the best. In the Black culture, there is a saying, "When you are Black, you have to be ten times better than others and then be expected to do even more." Facing the harsh realities in my professional career forced me to accept the fact that I needed to "self-coach."

I revisited my personal goals and aspirations. What was I really trying to accomplish? What were my goals? What was holding me back in my professional career? What could I have done differently to have achieved the "W?" I had to accept some realities that challenged my reasons for my pursuit. Had my goals been met? What did my "W" look like? I believed in the three goals established long ago as a little girl in Mississippi. First, I achieved the education. Second, I am an honest upright citizen. Finally, the third one, whatever I did, I did my best to be the best. Why was I feeling as though I had not achieved the "W?" As I assessed the original goals, I realized I had achieved all of the "W's" along the way in this journey. There was evidence of the "W" as I reached each milestone. I had all of the fundamental skills and capabilities necessary to be successful.

I slowly came to the realization that I had been achieving the "W" the entire time. I was a sub component of Mr. Floyd and Mrs. Earnestine's goals. The journey I was on did not mean everything I wanted to happen would happen. It meant that I would achieve the success in life where it mattered the most. I had clear direction that setting goals are important. Having goals and aspirations play a major role in shaping who we are and how we view the world. Having goals helps refocus when things don't go the way you had hoped. Rather, being goal oriented and having a process in place helps generate a positive attitude about failures and setbacks. These are temporary life interruptions and not permanent shutdowns.

When I assessed what had become my obsession, becoming a VP, or achieving the highest title for my chosen career, I realized I had not set goals for that specific outcome. When I revisited the three goals for success, I achieved the "W." First, the education goal, achieved. I have two Engineering degrees, a Bachelor, Masters and Doctorate degree. These education endeavors have helped me navigate my personal and professional life. My educational successes offered opportunities for me to encourage and motivate others on their educational journeys. Second, be an honest and upright citizen goal was met. There is no way to put a value on integrity and being viewed as someone who is an upright citizen. This sense of being fair and operating with integrity is invaluable. In business dealings, your ability to be ethical and responsible for living up to your commitments is crucial for success. Success is often times measured on how well you managed your family and finances. I have a beautiful family and friends who love and support me. In my community, I am counted on to help the less fortunate, and volunteer my time. Finally, whatever I did, I did my best to be the best. Therefore, the third goal was also achieved.

In essence, I have achieved the "W" many times and I am still in the game. I am a successful wife, mother, grand and great grandmother, family member, friend, entrepreneur, business owner, real estate owner and investor, community volunteer and a true believer in my religious convictions. I have done my best to be the best in every aspect of my personal life, education, career endeavors, personal accomplishments and achievements, financial stability, and I will leave a legacy for those I love.

In conclusion, life is not about a single focus or a single moment in time. Life is about a continuum of ups and downs, highs and lows, passing and failing. The total sum of all things is what defines success or failure. As I look back over my life's journey, I see many wins. I learned that when we narrow our focus to only see the thing you did not achieve, you may lose sight of all the things you have achieved. Focusing on a single loss should be used as a time to refocus and set your next goal. Having a broader perspective of your goals and refocusing your plan as needed is more important than getting stuck on one thing that didn't go as planned and not moving forward. If you ever feel defeated in one area, step away and assess the many "W's" you have achieved in all other areas of your life. Understanding that the game is not over and you are still in the game offers hope for achieving the "W." Ask yourself these questions:

1. Is my scope for success too narrow?

2. Do I have what I need to accomplish this goal?

3. Am I accepting the small "w" along the way to my big "W?"

About Dr. Mae Killebrew-Mosley

D_{r.} M_{ae} K_{illebrew-}M_{osley} has an extensive background in human resources management, certifications as a professional career coach, diversity and inclusion practitioner, employee relations, content developing and training facilitation. Dr. Killebrew-Mosley has held many executive roles in large and  mid-sized companies. She is a Mississippi native who moved to Wisconsin for education and career opportunities. She has a Doctorate degree in business administration, MBA in human resources, Bachelor's degree in communication and business, two engineering degrees and completed International Business Management and Leadership through Thunderbird University-France.

Dr. Killebrew-Mosley is a multifaceted professional with a wealth of knowledge and experience in consulting, small business development, cultural competencies, staffing efficiencies and nonprofits. Her business, Markets Demand More, LLC is a consulting service that provides operations and staff utilization based on Industrial Engineering techniques.

Dr. Killebrew-Mosley is a wife, mother, grandmother, and truly enjoys family by hosting huge gatherings in her home. She has coined the phrase, "Thanksmas," as a way of celebrating both holidays with family for those who cannot travel for both Thanksgiving and Christmas holidays. She also enjoys travel and formal fashion designing in her free time.

You can find Dr. Killebrew-Mosley on Facebook here: https://www.facebook.com/mdmhrconsulting

You can find Dr. Killebrew-Mosley on LinkedIn here: https://www.linkedin.com/in/mae-d-killebrew-mosley-d-b-a-baa385a/

The Transformational Journey

How I went from Burned Out and Busted to Aligning and Thriving

"If you decide to take this journey with me, you will learn, you will grow, and you will build the transformational muscles that allow you to easily navigate the changes and resistance that come with each new chapter in your life."

by Dr. Melissa Tanner, CPC®, MBTI®, RMT

Transformation is not easy. It is courageous, heart-centered, and satisfying, but never easy. Across the span of our life, we become many versions of ourselves and experience many transformational catalysts. Are you ready to step onto your next transformational path? If so, follow my story, and let me show you how.

I started my first transformational journey at 14 years old in a used bookstore with my mom. On this day, I spied a set of cassette tapes for $5 - Tony Robbins' Personal Power. My mom agreed to purchase the set for me. I listened to the recordings many times and kept them well into my mid-20s. I dreamt of impacting people's lives as his words did mine. Over the years, I was influenced by authors and coaches like Louise Hay, Wayne Dyer, Julia Cameron, and many others.

Fast forward to 2010, I was looking forward to a bright future as a business consultant and wanted to expand my coaching knowledge. I attended the Certified Professional Coach (CPC) training through the Wainwright Global Institute of Professional Coaching. It felt like I had finally made my dream come true! In the following ten years, I successfully worked with corporate organizations and individuals to help them transform, align, and shift to new realities. As I continued building my client list, I worked in corporate and collegiate environments as a full-time employee while earning my Doctorate in Education, specializing in Performance Improvement Leadership, Usui and Karuna Reiki Master Teacher Certification, and Myers-Briggs Personality Type Indicator Assessment and Interpreter ™(MBTI™) Certification.

The most powerful transformational journey of my life began in May 2021. I made the decision to leave corporate life and become a full-time coach. My corporate job, living through Category 5 Hurricane Michael, contracting COVID-19, and the resurgence of the grief surrounding my mother's death had left me "burnt out and busted" mentally, physically, and emotionally. When I returned from a 10-day vacation, I realized I was not rested and was still trying to manage my mental and physical well-being with little luck. The impacts of the pandemic were in full swing, and like many others, I was trying to adapt to the new way of working and living. Even though the company I worked for pivoted better than most, it was still not enough to find the balance I sought.

As a coach, I knew I had to start making changes to help me move forward. I started asking myself, "What substantial action would make the most impact in the largest number of areas of my life?" For me, that substantial action was to leave my corporate job and heal.

Lesson 1: You Need Community.

I was stretched to my limits, but I was healing. I needed a community.

Before leaving my corporate position, I found my soul-filling community in a group of healers, yogis, and beautiful people who helped me return to myself. Because of these people, I am a 200hr Registered Yoga Teacher (RYT200) and own a beautiful djembe drum. When the pandemic shutdown occurred, we were all scattered in the wind. The only remaining connection was through social media, which lacked human connection. I felt like I was losing myself and becoming a workaholic. I had to find a way to hold on to myself.

Lesson 2: Become your Own Best Friend.

As an introvert with an entrepreneurial spirit, my goal from the time I started working was to have my own company, to have the freedom to work when and where I wanted to work and to contribute to society in a meaningful way. The pandemic gave me the space, time, and opportunity to feel autonomy in a big way and to become my own best friend.

During this period, I was single and lived alone. My weekends and evenings were spent doing things I enjoyed versus commuting, grocery shopping, or doing housework. The early mornings and evenings were reserved for reading, cooking new recipes, practicing yoga, and journaling.

Lesson 3: Listen to Your Intuition.

As I was experiencing a transformation, autonomy, and authenticity personally, my work life became prescriptive and restrictive. Leadership was overworked and began micromanaging projects as they attempted to learn to manage remote employees. I had finished my doctorate less than six months earlier, yet I felt mistrusted, dull-witted, and undervalued. This was the opposite of the resilience I felt outside the workplace. Eventually, my body and mind gave me plenty of red flags. I was not sleeping, my face looked drawn and tired, and feelings of depression made themselves evident. My intuition, mental health, and body gave me the green light to run fast and far. I listened.

Lesson 4: Rest and Recovery is not a Luxury.

As I attempted to problem-solve, I networked across the organization for different roles and opportunities that might be a good fit for me. Unfortunately, there was not a place for me within my career path or other parts of the organization. Many people resigned, which resulted in unmanageable workloads and 12-hour workdays minimum. For me, burnout came more quickly and with a vengeance. I needed time to rest and recover. I resigned.

After completing my resignation notice period, the extra time and reduced stress allowed me to holistically heal my long-standing adrenal fatigue, enjoy my life, and complete the required home repairs from the hurricane. My home, my body, and my life were mine again.

I do not regret leaving my corporate role. I learned a lot of lessons, and I am still patting myself on the back for taking this leap of faith and putting myself first. During this 18-month sabbatical, I transformed my life.

Here is a brief list of the fun and work I did to align and thrive:

- Enjoyed the Forgotten Coast & got a tan.
- Taught multiple yoga classes a week.
- Hosted a live radio show called Counterbalance Conversations and launched the Counterbalance Coach website.
- Lunched, brunched, and spent time with friends and family without checking my phone.
- Took a 10-day vacation to North Carolina for my 50th birthday and saw fall colors.
- Certified 3 Reiki Master Teachers
- Took art classes. Basket weaving was my favorite!
- Meditated, Journaled, and explored shadow work & yoga.
- Designed and launched my 6-week Reclaiming Your Creativity class.
- Coached three people to make a leap out of corporate.
- Played my singing bowls & went to drum circles.
- Engaged with my inner child daily.
- Met AMAZING female authors (Hey Fab 5!)
- SMILED…A LOT MORE!
- Decided I wanted to write and help people heal for a living.

In my half-century of life, I have transformed into many iterations of myself and have gone through many stages of life. Each stage was beautiful and provided stepping stones to the happy, integrated, and whole self that I see in the mirror today. This transformation was, by far, my most impactful healing experience. As a result of this healing work, I now thrive in all areas of my life. I was able to attract a beautiful soul into my life, who is now my husband and, with him, my stepson. We have abundant happiness, love, support, dreams, and finances. Truthfully, our life is my dream come true. My coaching and healing business is rapidly expanding. To support this expansion, I will begin offering Certified Professional Coach training as a Master Coach of Wainwright Global Institute of Professional Coaching.

Do I still have work to do? YES! Was the journey worth it? YES! If you decide to take this journey with me, you will learn, you will grow, and you will build the transformational muscles that allow you to easily navigate the changes and resistance that come with each new chapter in your life. As a transformation coach, I am responsible for asking you the right questions, providing you with tools, pointing you in the right direction, and being your accountability partner on the path to your dream life. If you are ready to align and thrive like I have, I invite you to take this journey with me!

I would love to work with you and help you Align and Thrive!

To join my mailing list, if you think I would be a good fit for you as a coach or would like to share your thoughts about this chapter, go to SparkUHealing.com/book and drop me a note.

When you reach out or join my mailing list, you will receive a 30-minute complementary conversation directly with me, Dr. Tanner.

Remember to connect with me on Facebook and Instagram: @SparkUHealing

About Dr. Melissa Tanner, CPC®, MBTI®, RMT

D_{r.} M_{elissa} T_{anner} is the CEO of Counterbalance Visionaries, LLC and SparkU Healing, LLC. Her favorite accomplishment is helping individuals align and thrive through holistic practices, including coaching, shadow work, inner child work, Reiki, and mindfulness.

She has an Ed.D. in Performance Improvement Leadership and a Master's Degree in Aeronautical Science with a Specialization in Aviation/Aerospace Education Technology. She holds certifications as an MBTI® Administrator and Interpreter, a Certified Professional Coach, and a 200-hour Yoga Teacher.

In 2021, Dr. Tanner left the corporate world to work full-time as a coach, an educator, and a resilience champion. After leaving her corporate engagement, Dr. Tanner expanded her coaching to include corporate consulting and has an impressive resume of real-world experience working with corporate clients in the areas of culture, leadership, and employee development.

Dr. Tanner lives on the Emerald Coast of Florida with her husband, son, and two dogs. In her free time, she teaches yoga, goes to the beach, reads, and enjoys family time.

Contact information for Dr. Tanner:

Dr. Melissa Tanner, CPC®, MBTI®, RMT

Founder, SparkU Healing and Yoga

850.596.8554

SparkUHealing@gmail.com

Coaching has parted the clouds!

Coaching has brought positivity and growth to myself as well as my clients.

"If you decide to take this journey with me, you will learn, you will grow, and you will build the transformational muscles that allow you to easily navigate the changes and resistance that come with each new chapter in your life."

by Phil Chabot

It was the summer of 2006. The climate in Detroit was hot and humid with an immense amount of economic uncertainty in practically every headline, news story, or water cooler conversation. Those in the know were comforted by their feeling of being set in life with career choices made with advantages enjoyed. For those feeling skeptical, like me, these were perilous times as uncertainty was found in every aspect of life, business or personal.

Since I began working well before my sixteenth birthday, I practiced what my parents instilled in us (I'm the youngest of six kids) when in public/at work: Treat everyone as equals whether they push a broom or run a company. Over the years, this became my go-to approach with everyone which was appreciated and rewarded with career opportunities and advancement. It seemed that all I had to do was show up and everything would work out positively for me. Unfortunately, this was about to change in a big way.

I had spent over twelve years in the automotive industry as a front-line application engineer for everything related to an assembly line worker to presenting solutions both mechanical and ergonomic to upper management and being rewarded with purchasing agreements that made my competitors green with envy. I felt like I had found my career (life) niche. I became a specialist and went on to become a Certified Ergonomics Technician and authored a master's Thesis on Ergonomics in the Workplace: Ergonomics as it pertains to worker positioning and required task(s). I rose to Vice President of a power tool manufacturer and brought improved health and productivity to assembly line workers everywhere. Whether it was automotive, aerospace, foundry, or general industry, I could bring solution(s) that benefitted all parties concerned.

Life was good.

Then came "The Call" one Friday afternoon. I was reviewing my recent communications and was preparing for the next week's travels and demonstrations when my phone rang. It was the main office number (I worked remotely, roughly three hours from HQ). I answered thinking that the President had forgotten to update me on something, which often happened to us both over the years. He seemed coy, somewhat reserved. I asked if everything was ok. He responded yes but had some news for me. My base salary was being cut 50% effective immediately. After returning my jaw to its normal position, I asked if there was anything that I could do to stave off such a drastic move? He responded that there was not. I accepted his decision and signed off. What followed was a roller coaster ride that I wasn't expecting yet looking back, it was the best thing that could have happened to me. It was December 30, 2008.

Shortly after receiving the call, my wife and I went to our favorite bar/micro-brewery for their Friday Happy Hour and enjoyed their killer Long Island Iced Teas and mountainous, multi-level cheeseburgers and jalapeno poppers. It was at this moment of euphoric enjoyment that I sprang the news to my wife about the 50% pay cut. Without saying a word, she topped off our drinks from the pitcher of Long Islands, raised her glass and asked, "What is your plan?" I responded that I was going back to school as I wanted to become more valuable to society in preparation for the next economic downturn. I wanted to pursue a graduate degree in psychology that utilized my commercial success so that I could draw on my experience, perhaps have an easier program than a novice. It was a dinner of celebration rather than defeat.

I awakened the next morning with a slight hangover (it could have been much worse had I not downed a glass of water and a few aspirin). The sun was up and my dog, Jac, was ready for some quality Dad time. This was delayed by Mom who had the family computer on and had navigated to The Chicago School's homepage and handed me my weekend coffee special which included a shot of Bailey's. At that moment, I knew that my life would never be the same.

By Monday morning, I had formally applied and submitted my entrance essay to attend The Chicago School in pursuit of a master's degree in Industrial and Organizational

Psychology. Over the next eighteen months, my work travels included both a work laptop and school laptop, both of which saw use every day. I was either assessing a workspace for ergonomics or delving into the psychological landscape of manufacturing every waking moment. I remember thinking how much I looked forward to completing my degree and elevating my personal knowledge where few had explored, especially in the manufacturing sector.

In the months that led up to my completing my degree, I realized that my talents were misdirected towards corporations rather than individuals. It seemed that my focus on worker ergonomics allowed organizations to adjust both workspace and workload and squeezed the worker for output/productivity with no regard for the person behind the power tool or keyboard. Oh, and they had no use for me once [their] solutions were put in place. I felt used. Empty.

During one of our Saturday morning nature walks with our white German Shepherd, Jac, I shared with my wife that I wasn't content with achieving my I/O Psychology degree and wanted to pursue something that would help the forgotten factory worker or ignored office worker, regardless of industry. I wanted to bring positivity to everyone without the filter or control of an organization or corporation. But how? I was wrapping up a graduate program and did not see myself enrolling in another degree program.

By that Sunday evening, I had found Fowler Wainwright International Professional Coaching (now Wainwright Global Institute of Professional Coaching) online and upon exploring their website and most importantly, reading their testimonials, I decided to enroll in their program. Concerns of misalignment or selecting a program that may dilute my beliefs rather than augment them soon dissipated. From the introductions to exercises, to homework and roundtable discussions, the Fowler Wainwright program was spot-on with its messages, tools, and techniques. I was a new man.

Life was good.

It's Fall of 2010. I am now armed with a Coaching Certificate in addition to a Psychology Degree and thirty years of sales experience. Where will I go? What will be my focus?

Over the next five years, I worked diligently with my team to build a successful business rooted in developing cutting-edge products focused on the health of workers resulting in higher corporate profits. My personal involvement in worker questionnaire creation and soft skill solutions were unmatched by our competition. It became clear. We were doing what no one else was. We were listening to the worker and offering guidance in support of their goals. We were the teammate that everyone found supportive and helpful.

Life was good.

Unfortunately, this was short-lived as corporate profits began to shrink, due to other factors, which caused a shift in focus away from the worker and toward return on investment. The classic management style of the 1950's was rampant in some markets with expressed non-interest in our worker-centered programs. This triggered a thorough review of all products and services offered and the resulting revenue in each market. Upon completion, the future became clear. The business was to be product based and the support programs for the worker were to be provided only if the corporation requested them. No exceptions.

The writing was on the wall, so to speak, for me to look in the mirror and decide what it was that I felt passionate about and could it "stand alone" as a valued option for individuals seeking professional assistance in navigating their future, both personal and professional. I felt that with all that I had experienced throughout my career, both scholastically and professionally, my knowledge pool was quite deep in several areas, especially those relating to the human spirit and involvement in society. I was convinced that it was time for a change.

It's February 1, 2016. I have parted ways with my employer and have launched A Focused Approach, LLC offering individual and organizational coaching as well as I/O Psychology services.

To date, the most sought-after service has been individual coaching. This comes as no surprise as we all can benefit with an extra set of eyes (and ears) on whatever challenge(s) may be present, especially from a seasoned professional coach with a storied background of sales and psychology.

Life is good.

What do you feel passionate about that could alter your life and career trajectory in a positive way?

About Phil Chabot

Phil Chabot helps people find their compass in life and business. In doing so, identifying obstacles, and developing strategies for success become the playbook for all clients regardless of their goals or aspirations. Let's work together to achieve personal growth, happiness, and fulfillment in life!

Services Offered: Team Building • Training • Life Coaching • Public Speaking • Leadership Development • Diversity & Inclusion • Career Development Coaching

Learn more about Phil Chabot by visiting his LinkedIn profile: www.linkedin.com/in/philipchabot/

Send Phil your inquiry here: coachphil52@hotmail.com

Ctrl + Alt + Delete

Reset Your Mind. Reset Your Life!

"L.O.V.E. - Listen. Observe. Validate. Explore."

"By limiting acceptance for what we feel our past life did to us, we are then limiting the opportunity of present & future growth for what life has to offer us."

by Coach Stefan Rudolph

Passion. Power. Purpose. The "Command to Expand" is what I had in life for life through life with life…all in order to end the "old life" and begin the "new life!" I had to set free the desire to grow and use it as fuel to "believe the unbelievable, achieve the unachievable and conceive the inconceivable." Here I found that the "challenges" of life should be followed by the necessary "changes" in life in order to grow…as "change" is a part of "challenge":

CHA-lle-NGE

Upon my personal shift and change in life as sobriety and growth entered my life, I experienced a turning point that I termed… "The Holy Shift!" A point where I had to become "less with my past life and more with my future life daily". Here I had to accept, forgive, learn and grow. I had to "rise wise in order to face the tides" of life by giving up on the past, as the past had now passed as I developed the strength to give up on the "old me" in order to grow the "new me".

Yet this "old me" did not want to give up! Every day that went by was filled with excuses to look back and try to achieve what I once had in life, what I had lost in life and what I once was in life. These excuses kept me in the past and never let the past pass. Here I found that the "inability" to have the "capability" to perceive the "ability" to change is what nearly killed me. It wasn't what I did in the "past" that brought me down; it was what I was doing in the "present to remain in the past" that never got me out of the "old me". Now is where I needed to "face it in order to erase it!"

I had to believe, perceive and receive the unachievable by starting my new path of growth from the inside out and saying, "Yes! I can!" All this, versus the previously repetitive: "Shouldn't, Couldn't and Wouldn't" that ruled my past life's path fueled by excuses from the "old me" that nearly ended me. Yet still, along the way, the closeness of ending my life happened multiple times and brought me down to near death by living in "insanity!"

Then, the passion, the fuel, the purpose, the desire, the ambition to not give up is what took my life to the next level. My life was now fueled by the heart of passion and connected with the mind of action, all in order to break the rule of the Ego who spent years filling me with blame, all in order to "remain the same". Yet then I saw how I had to travel down the long road of forgiveness as I found I could no longer use excuses of the past that kept me in the past.

Still, I had to "Face it. Embrace it. Acknowledge it and Replace it!" Overcoming this F.E.A.R. in me to change was the hardest shift I ever made. Every time the anxiety hit, the depression hit, the fear hit, the "old me" wanted to drink more, fail more, blame more and eventually die as it knew my past life was over! Here I had to recognize stillness, recognize thoughts, recognize actions and then, begin to recognize results. Here I had to refrain from excuses; refrain from blame and retrain my mind to connect the dots of thoughts and "eliminate in between the heart and the mind…the mouth full of excuses!"

Here I found, understood and implemented these steps: "Give yourself five seconds of healing. Give yourself five seconds of grace. Give yourself five seconds of feeling and give yourself five seconds of faith." And here I began to look for the "Father Above" that I needed in order to grow into a new life, as for the "father below" who brought me into this world was never there for me in my life. Then at this shifting point for me, the anger, resentment and negativity that I once had in my drinking days…had now vanished in my sober days.

I came to understand that those in our past don't always have to be there in our present if there is no love involved for our future. I saw this now and I thanked what are called the "Naysayers!" The naysayers were so-called friends or drinking buddies that wanted me back in their old life, to be like I was and to fail like I used to fail in life. But I now saw that the inability to think outside of the box will "end-ability" to ever truly live and truly grow in life. This is what I understood, accepted and changed. I now had a story of heart and passion from being in 14 years of "Lockdown" due to alcoholism, epilepsy and overall

Escapism from life. The steps to this change, shift and growth all became my book entitled "Thank You to the 1,000th Power!" A story of opening the mind and creating a spiritual connectivity to the heart for the fuel of addiction and excuses to leave me.

During this time as sobriety entered my life in 2012, I had now finished a 10-year run of "chasing death to the finish line" life that included four DUI's, six weeks in jail, multiple car accidents, along with a pulmonary embolism, four endoscopies, 25+ years of epilepsy from a high school football injury, brain surgery that did not work, divorce, jail, homelessness, the list went on. I had every reason to die in life, but at this point, I had every reason to live a new life.

I began to ask God Himself above in my life for help to "uncover, recover and discover" a whole new life. And then through the challenges and changes I survived through and grew through in life, I was given the power to help others through my book to fuel their own life for growth. This is what I had gone through and grew through in life after surviving 42 days or that being the equivalent of a total of just over 1,000 hours in jail. So now, "I was done being done!" and was a new man who "knew" now how to "blame less and gain more."

"By limiting acceptance for what we feel our past life did to us, we are then limiting the opportunity of present and future growth for what life has to offer us."

Now, upon my awakening, I saw in the past how my pain was self-chosen by fueling myself with alcohol and escapism. I was at a shifting point and a growth point in life where I accepted life for what it was in my past and where I was now in my present. I accepted all that I had been through and survived through and ended all thoughts of what I felt I "should have" been previously. And then, sobriety hit, growth hit and a shifting point hit as I began to master the moment of "Now". Here I saw how if I own the "Own the moment of Now, I will have Won the moment of life." Now, Own, Won (N.O.W.), this helped me to realize that the "acceptance of negativity" was actually extreme "Fuel for Growth!"

I now saw how choosing emotions was my choice. Either choosing the ruling figure of "Passion" for life, such as love for life in my heart, or choosing the draining figure of "fear and evil" for life from my mind that was living in me; here at this point, both were my choice. A choice to either live in love, or live in fear. Fear of which I now saw was defined through the acronyms of "Fuel for Escapism Against Reality". This was the fear created when I drank alcohol, gambled, partied and fueled myself in overall "Escapism" against reality and ended up in jail and nearly dead.

And then 7 years later in the "7 Year Shift" or the "Holy Shift" in my life, right in the middle of "Lock Down" I knew here that there was an ear to hear my story, my book and my comeback in life and to be an inspiration to others to never give up and be able to understand the "command to expand" begins within you for you through you by you, all in order to grow your "new self, new being and new spirit for life!" So go now and grow now and take your life to the next level and may this chapter help you... "Turn the F' You's to Thank You's" in life forever more!

In the end, I come to you today to bring you a story of passion, a story of purpose, a story of heart, a story of freedom, a story of "lockdown", and a story of opening the mind to connect with the heart and eliminate that busy mouth full of excuses in between. All along this journey as you read my book, you will see how "Thank you to the 1,000th Power" provides a deeper understanding of how you should look "within yourself" for change and growth and "take a bold chance to make a dramatic change" by first seeing the "chance in change" and the "change in challenge" when you take the necessary growth steps to action in life!

So go now and grow now and awaken today on this journey of your new life in order to bring yourself to a new enlightenment of finding the true "new you" by first finding the "truth of forgiveness." All this by knowing that "what you serve out in life, you will receive back in life" and that "fear is not on the outside of you, it is on the inside of you." So, we must create the necessary steps and change to face these obstacles and use them as fuel for growth. That is where this book, this new path and what you have in front of you today, that being the bold courage of love for a new life will help you listen, observe, validate & explore the option of creating a new life, all through the fuel of "Love for Life."

About Stefan Rudolph

Coach Stefan Rudolph is a motivational speaker, author, life coach, epilepsy coach and entrepreneur. His experience in overcoming obstacles in life includes a 25-year battle with epilepsy and alcoholism combined with surviving multiple related car accidents, a pulmonary embolism and brain surgery. This is a story of heartfelt hope and passion for  the reader who is looking to grow and expand after experiencing their own *"Lock Down"* journey in life.

Stefan discusses his 14-year battle of being *"Locked Up, Locked In, Locked Out and Locked Down"* in life due to alcoholism, epilepsy, gambling and overall escapism in life. From one year living the *"American Dream Lifestyle"*, being happily married with a six-figure income in the pharmaceutical industry, to suddenly facing brain surgery, bankruptcy, divorce, jail and homelessness.

This is an inspirational story of love for life and never giving up on life that will capture the reader by showing the steps he took during the hardest times for turning the *"Survive into Thrive"* by *"turning the impossible into I'm Possible!"* All this by never giving in and never giving up in life through passion, courage and strength in order to make the ultimate *"Rocky Balboa"* comeback in life!

"L.O.V.E. - Listen. Observe. Validate. Explore."

To Your Health, Wellness and Personal Growth,

Coach Stefan Rudolph

YouTube, Facebook & Instagram: Coach Stefan Rudolph

Book info: www.ThankYou1000.com

Audible and Spotify: www.CommandToExpand.com

Speaking: www.MotivationalSpeakingForGrowth.com

Coaching: www.RecoveredCoaching.com

Email: info@RecoveredCoaching.com

Call/Text: 760-215-2337

Bridging Estrangement: Always Invite and Embrace Coaching and Feedback ... it works.

"Feedback is like a fresh breeze, clearing away fog, smoke, and haziness to reveal clarity and understanding."

"The combination of active and empathetic listening with quality feedback creates a powerful engine for transformation."

by James A. White, Sr.

A highly educated male friend with military experience and brilliant writing skills approached me with a heartfelt request: "Would you assist me in developing a more meaningful connection with my two estranged adult sons?" Thus, our journey began. For a year, we met in my living room every Wednesday around 6 pm to embark on this important endeavor.

Before we began, I asked him one crucial question: "Are you ready to respond to the challenging questions and pushback you might receive from your sons?" I reminded him that they could be carrying a tremendous amount of pain and anguish from years of growing up without his presence and guidance. He assured me he was prepared to absorb whatever they might direct at him. I admired his openness and receptivity, even to painful and sometimes hostile questions.

Initially, only his oldest son was open to coaching with his father. Each week, the two of them engaged in dialogue, debate, and discussion. On several occasions, the energy and passion were both real and meaningful. They talked and exchanged thoughts, feelings, hurts, and pains, allowing hidden discomforts to finally surface in search of clarity. Through these intense and emotional conversations, powerful breakthroughs were achieved. Together, they have authored a book, with my assistance coaching about their life journey, illustrating the powerful connections they maintained despite geographical separation.

My role as a coach and friend was to facilitate healthy exchanges, moving forward one step at a time, addressing one pain at a time, and uncovering one heartfelt discovery at a time. A key point I must share is that the lynchpin and or keystone of personal and professional growth and development in their exchange was the father's unwavering openness to feedback. No matter how difficult or emotionally assaulting it was, he always invited and embraced it. Being open, receptive, and inviting feedback is critical for growth, problem-solving, resolution, and reunion to become a reality. As all this unfolded, we continued to meet in my living room, fostering an environment where healing and reconnection were possible. These sessions allowed them to address deep-seated issues, rebuild trust, and develop a more meaningful and heartfelt connection. The journey was transformative, not only strengthening their relationship but also contributing to their individual growth and understanding.

It also involves recognizing and reinforcing what is working well. Positive feedback boosts confidence, motivation, and morale, encouraging individuals to continue their efforts and strive for excellence. It provides validation and acknowledgment of the progress made, which is critical for sustaining momentum and commitment to the coaching process. In my coaching practice, I emphasize the importance of creating a feedback-rich environment where open and honest communication was encouraged and valued. This involves setting clear expectations from the outset about the role of feedback and establishing a safe space where clients feel comfortable sharing their thoughts and experiences without fear of judgment or criticism.

The feedback sessions were structured to ensure they were constructive and actionable. We focus on specific behaviors and outcomes rather than personal attributes, which helps to depersonalize the feedback and make it more impactful. Techniques such as the "SBI" (Situation-Behavior-Impact) model is used to frame feedback clearly and focused, providing concrete examples and the context needed for understanding and improvement. Furthermore, I integrate regular feedback loops into the coaching process. This ongoing dialogue allows for real-time adjustments and ensures that the coaching remains aligned with the client's evolving needs and goals. It also helps to build a culture of continuous improvement, where both successes and setbacks are viewed as opportunities for learning and growth.

Throughout our year-long journey, the transformation extended beyond just the father and his sons reconnecting; it had a profound impact on everyone's personal growth and emotional intelligence. Each session was a blend of structured activities and organic conversations, designed to elicit deep emotional responses and foster genuine understanding. In addition to active listening exercises, we incorporated role-playing scenarios where the father and his sons would switch roles to see the world from each other's perspectives. This exercise was particularly enlightening, as it allowed them to walk in each other's shoes and better appreciate the challenges and experiences they each faced. It was through these role reversals that they began to see humanity in each other, leading to greater empathy and compassion. We also utilized journaling as a tool for reflection. Each of them kept a journal where they could express their thoughts and feelings in between sessions. This practice helped them process their emotions privately and articulate their experiences more clearly during our meetings. The father, being a brilliant writer, found this exercise particularly therapeutic. His written reflections often served as a springboard for deeper conversations in our sessions. The breakthrough moments were numerous and powerful. One session stands out when the father openly apologized for his past absences and the pain it caused. This act of vulnerability broke down significant barriers, allowing his sons to see his regret and genuine desire to make amends. This heartfelt apology was a pivotal moment that shifted the dynamics of their relationship, paving the way for forgiveness and healing.

As their relationship strengthened, as previously stated, they began to collaborate on a book about their life's journey. This project was not just a recounting of their experiences but a profound exploration of their emotional landscapes. Authoring the book together provided them with a shared goal and a sense of accomplishment. It also served as a lasting testament to their journey of reconciliation and growth.

The combination of active and empathetic listening with quality feedback creates a powerful engine for transformation. It enables clients to gain deeper insights into their behaviors and mindsets, fosters greater self-awareness, and promotes an initiative-taking approach to personal and professional development. By embracing feedback as a core component of the coaching journey, clients are better equipped to navigate challenges, seize opportunities, and achieve lasting success and reconciliation in all areas of their lives. In summary, the deliberate and skillful use of feedback in coaching sessions is a crucial element that can significantly enhance the effectiveness of the coaching experience. It empowers clients to understand and address the root causes of their challenges, facilitates meaningful dialogue, and drives continuous improvement. By prioritizing feedback, coaches can help clients unlock their full potential and achieve their highest aspirations.

As a result of my 35-plus years of training and coaching across a diverse array of businesses, organizations, government agencies, K-12 schools, and colleges and universities, I have embraced and validated that the skill and power of coaching is the single most powerful tool that can be adopted and employed to influence and inspire friends, associates, and clients. This realization has been the cornerstone of my professional journey, guiding me in refining my coaching methodologies and maximizing their impact. Through mastering over thirteen training initiatives and earning five coaching certifications, and through my interactions and engagements with thousands of clients, I have come to understand that coaching is not just an effective tool, but the most essential component in my arsenal.

Active and empathetic listening, on the other hand, is the foundation of a successful coaching relationship. It involves fully engaging with clients, understanding their perspectives, and acknowledging their emotions. This practice fosters a sense of trust and respect, creating a safe environment where clients feel valued and heard. By listening actively and empathetically, coaches can uncover the underlying issues that clients may face and help them navigate their challenges with greater ease and confidence. The combination of being open to feedback and mastering active listening forms a powerful duo that significantly enhances the coaching experience. These skills are not only valuable in professional settings but also in personal life.

I have found immense value in applying these principles with my own family, especially with my ten adult grandchildren and my growing nine great-grandchildren. The ability to listen empathetically and provide constructive feedback has helped me build stronger, more meaningful relationships with them, fostering an environment of mutual respect and understanding. In my coaching practice, I strive to create a feedback-rich environment where open communication is encouraged. I set clear expectations about the role of feedback and establish a safe space for sharing thoughts and experiences. Feedback sessions were structured to be constructive and actionable, focusing on specific behaviors and outcomes rather than personal attributes. This approach helps to depersonalize feedback, making it more impactful and easier to act upon.

In conclusion, the skills of being open to feedback and practicing active and empathetic listening are paramount in coaching. These skills not only enhance the effectiveness of the coaching experience but also drive continuous improvement and meaningful connections. Embracing these principles in both professional and personal life leads to lasting, positive change, ensuring that success is always attainable.

About James A. White, Sr.

James A. White Sr. is a Master Training Management Consultant and executive coach with over 40 years of corporate, education, and government training and development experience. He is currently the owner of Performance Consulting Services, a 34-year-old business performance training, development, coaching, inclusion and emotional intelligence, diversity, and consulting firm in Columbus. James served in United States Air Force, in the capacities of Air Police Officer and a Top Security Draftsman. He worked for three highly reputable, international corporations including Digital Equipment Corporation, Wang Laboratories and Xerox Corporation in sales and training. Jim holds two degrees and has acquired over thirty certifications in professional performance development, coaching with executives, staff and personal independent citizens, small groups and organizations. He has also accumulated tens of thousands of hours of platform delivery experience in classrooms, workshops and seminars. Professional highlights include, co-authoring a book entitled; A Better World: A Framework for Diversity, Inclusion and Engagement and he is an

International TedTalk Speaker: James A. White Sr. - Ted Talk Columbus, Ohio.

Jim is committed to an inclusive approach to the growth, development, and advancement of all people. He believes that every person and organization has incredible potential. He works to help them understand it — and communicate it to others.

See his Ted Talk here:

https://www.ted.com/speakers/james_a_white_sr

You can reach James here:

performanceconsultingtrainingservices.com

jwhite2@columbus.rr.com

614-562-3372

From Personal Challenges to Passion

My journey, marked by both struggles and triumphs, is a testament to hope, determination, and the transformative power of compassion

"With the right support, anyone can navigate their way through life's challenges and come out stronger on the other side."

by Gilda Simonét

I often wonder how my coaching could affect my clients' lives. This isn't just a random thought; it's a concern that stays with me. Growing up, I faced a lot of challenges. Life had its tough moments, and I had to figure out how to handle them early on. These experiences made me want to help others navigate their paths.

As a kid, I was the friend who always listened when others were going through rough patches. Helping them see things more clearly and giving advice that helped felt amazing. These moments have planted the seed for my passion for life coaching. I knew firsthand how overwhelming life's challenges could be, and I wanted to offer the support I often needed myself. As I went through my journey, I met many people stuck in cycles of doubt and fear, just like I had been. Seeing this made me want to help others break free and realize their potential. If I could overcome my obstacles, they could too.

When I started my career as a life coach, I knew every client would be different, each with their own stories and struggles. I couldn't use a one-size-fits-all approach. Instead, I dedicated myself to understanding each person's fears and dreams and tailored my guidance to help meet their specific needs. Watching clients transform, gaining confidence, and tackling their goals with new energy, strengthened my sense of purpose. My mission has remained clear: to help others change their lives, just like I had changed mine.

Lessons in Perseverance

Growing up with deaf parents, my world was a unique blend of silence and sound. My earliest memories include the graceful movements of American Sign Language (ASL), my parents' expressive faces, and the constant noise of a world I was learning to interpret for them. At home, communication was an art form.

Life at school was a different story. The responsibilities I carried were often overwhelming for my age. While other kids were carefree, I was navigating adult-level challenges, interpreting at doctor's appointments or during parent-teacher conferences. This often left me feeling misunderstood and isolated, steering me down a troubled path in my teens as I searched for a sense of belonging.

Everything changed when I met a mentor who believed in me. They saw beyond my troubled exterior and helped me see that there was more to life than the path I was on. They introduced me to new experiences and perspectives, which helped me to discover strengths I didn't know I had.

Gilda Simonét

Through their guidance, I realized that my unique experiences had equipped me with empathy and resilience.

My journey, marked by both struggles and triumphs, is a testament to hope, determination, and the transformative power of compassion.

Having deaf parents taught me a lot about the barriers to communication and the importance of empathy. These experiences, along with other personal challenges I faced, deeply influenced my understanding of resilience. Guiding others through their fears and aspirations forced me to confront my uncertainties. Could I support people in their emotional struggles? Were my words and guidance impactful enough to bring about real change? Amidst the doubts, there were moments of clarity and small victories. Each time I helped someone regain confidence or navigate tough decisions, it felt like a personal win.

Reflecting on those early days, I realized that being a life coach goes beyond just teaching skills. It's about embracing vulnerability, practicing empathy, and navigating challenges together with clients. These experiences deepened my appreciation for resilience and the profound value of genuine human connections.

Through all this, I learned that true coaching is about connecting on a human level. It's about understanding and sharing in the struggles and triumphs of others. My upbringing, my relationship with my deaf parents, and the personal challenges I faced, shaped this understanding and fueled my passion. Helping others change their lives has been both a challenge and a reward, reinforcing my belief that we all have the power to overcome our obstacles and achieve our dreams.

Empathy, Resilience, and Personalized Guidance

Throughout this journey, I've learned several important lessons. These lessons became the foundation that allowed me to move forward with confidence.

Firstly, I learned the power of empathy. Growing up with the kind of life I lived taught me how crucial it is to truly understand and connect with others. This understanding helped me build strong relationships with my clients and offer them the support they needed.

Secondly, I discovered the importance of resilience. Life threw many challenges my way, and overcoming them showed me that perseverance is key. This lesson inspired me to help my clients find their own strength and keep pushing forward, no matter how tough things get.

Lastly, I recognized the value of personalized guidance. Everyone's journey is different, and there's no one-size-fits-all approach. By really listening to my clients and tailoring my advice to their unique situations, I was able to have a real impact on their lives.

These three lessons--empathy, resilience, and personalized guidance--shaped my approach to coaching and helped me become a better coach. They also reinforced my belief that with the right support, anyone can overcome their obstacles and achieve their dreams.

Addressing these key elements--empathy, resilience, and personalized guidance--allowed me to prosper as a life coach. These principles supported me as I moved from a state of uncertainty to one of confidence and effectiveness in my role. They enabled me to make a meaningful impact on the lives of my clients, helping them to overcome their obstacles and reach their full potential. It's clear that my journey was not just about professional growth but also about personal transformation.

Each lesson learned and each client helped reinforce my commitment to this path. The process of becoming a life coach was filled with its own challenges and rewards, but it was these foundational principles that guided me through and allowed me to truly make a difference.

These experiences have shown me that with the right support, anyone can navigate their way through life's challenges and come out stronger on the other side. It's a journey of growth, resilience, and ultimately, transformation. And it's a journey I'm honored to be a part of, both for myself and for the clients I have the privilege of coaching.

About Gilda Simonét

Gilda Simonét is a certified life coach with a passion for helping others navigate their personal, spiritual, and professional journeys. Her mission is to empower individuals to overcome obstacles, achieve their goals, and realize their full potential. In addition to her coaching practice, Gilda dedicates her time to working with inner-city  kids, guiding them toward a better life through mentorship and support. This work is incredibly rewarding for her, as it allows her to make a meaningful impact on the next generation, instilling confidence and hope in young minds.

Additionally, Gilda co-hosts a podcast inspired by the teachings of Eckhart Tolle, where she explores concepts of mindfulness, presence, and personal growth. Through this platform, she aims to spread Tolle's transformative ideas to a broader audience, encouraging listeners to embrace a more conscious and fulfilling way of living.

Gilda's diverse experiences and dedication to personal development shape her approach to coaching, fostering a holistic and empathetic environment for her clients and mentees. Whether through one-on-one sessions, her podcast, or helping others in general, Gilda is committed to inspiring positive change and helping others lead empowered lives. Her work reflects her belief in the power of hope, determination, and compassion to create lasting change.

You can email Gilda Simonét here:

CoachingWithGilda@gmail.com

Her Podcast: "The Power of Now - A Guide to Spiritual Enlightenment with Gilda and Barbara" has garnered over 800,000 downloads on Spotify and is now broadcast on KPHRED.com and KAPY Radio.

Guiding Stars - The Fusion of Astrology and Life Coaching

Guiding individuals through their celestial blueprints and witnessing their transformations is not merely a career but a calling

"From the moment I gazed through a telescope at a luminescent night sky, a seed of fascination with the cosmos was planted in my heart"

by Mary Trimble

From the moment I gazed through a telescope at a luminescent night sky, a seed of fascination with the cosmos was planted in my heart. Little did I know that this intrigue would evolve into a lifelong passion, leading me to combine the ancient, mystical wisdom of astrology with the transformative power of life coaching. My journey has been a tapestry woven with stories of inspiration, challenges, and the unyielding belief in every individual's potential to steer their life toward fulfillment.

The Journey Begins:

Growing up, I was always curious about the world beyond the tangible. The stars, planets, and cosmic phenomena called my name. My initial foray into astrology was rooted in pure fascination—a hobby that quickly became a significant aspect of my identity. I immersed myself in studying astrological charts, lunar cycles, and the intricate dance of celestial bodies, discovering a profound connection with my inner self and the world around me.

Despite this deep connection with the cosmos, I found myself navigating the practical demands of a career that offered little soul satisfaction. I pursued a conventional path driven by societal expectations and the need for financial stability. Yet, the tug of my passion for astrology never waned, encouraging me to seek a balance between the material and the ethereal.

The Integration:

The turning point came during a period of personal upheaval. Confronting a crossroads in my career and questioning the very essence of my purpose, I turned to astrology for clarity. Delving deeper into my natal chart, I unearthed insights about my strengths, challenges, and potential life path. This introspection not only provided clarity but empowered me to pivot towards a more meaningful vocation.

The idea of merging astrology with life coaching was life-changing for me. While astrology could illuminate the hidden aspects of one's personality and destiny, life coaching offered the practical tools to manifest this potential. The fusion of these two disciplines emerged as a holistic approach where one could gain profound self-awareness through astrology and channel this insight into tangible actions through coaching.

A Story of Transformation:

One inspiring example of an extraordinary personal transformation involves a client we'll refer to as Mandy. When Mandy first approached me, she was overwhelmed by anxiety and indecision. Her business was on the brink of collapse, and she faced significant financial and personal debt. Additionally, Mandy was still grappling with the grief from her father's passing a couple of years earlier. Mandy's emotional turmoil was exacerbated by her persistent attachment to her childhood home, which she couldn't afford. Despite her family's need to sell the property to alleviate financial strain, Mandy sabotaged several potential sales, unable to let go of the past.

We started Mandy's journey with an in-depth analysis of her natal chart, which laid the groundwork for understanding her personality, challenges, and karmic lessons. Her North Node in Sagittarius suggested a life path oriented towards spirituality, exploration, and freedom. The Sun conjunct Neptune in her chart indicated profound creative, spiritual, and ideological inclinations. Mandy's chart also revealed a tendency to hold on to people, things, and outdated notions.

Understanding the urgency of addressing her financial challenges, we focused first on Mandy's openness to finding a part-time paid position. Despite initial resistance, Mandy recognized the necessity of a stable income while preserving the flexibility to pursue her creative passions.

Our coaching sessions were intrinsically linked to astrological insights. We developed strategies that merged Mandy's creative interests with her professional goals, leveraging auspicious astrological transits to determine optimal times for action. With newfound confidence and clarity, Mandy secured a position managing a luxurious rooftop lounge for the summer. Analyzing her chart, we determined that this role would be beneficial, providing independence with the necessary income without a long-term commitment and giving her the space to focus on her artistic passions. This experience led to valuable networking opportunities and a fulfilling summer position, which she returned to the following year.

Mandy's transformation was gradual but profound. She transitioned from managing a failing business with a fatalistic outlook to thriving in a social, temporary role that gave her freedom and enabled her to promote her creative projects.

A Lesson Learned:

Through continued coaching, Mandy's ultimate dream materialized—a beautiful home with a pool in a sunny location. This significant milestone was achieved within three years of our collaborative efforts. Her clear vision, nurtured through coaching, manifested her dream life. When it came time to move, we consulted her solar return chart, which indicated significant delays with Saturn on her ascendant. I advised her to delay the move until November to avoid expensive complications. We discussed the value of organizing and preparing for the move. However, Mandy was so confident in her manifesting powers that she believed she could make the move happen sooner. Her goal was to leave by the end of August.

Contrary to her chart's projections, Mandy took control and pushed forward with the move. Not surprisingly, she met with catastrophe after catastrophe. Her boyfriend had an accident playing sports and severely hurt his hand, which meant he couldn't lift heavy things or drive the truck. As a result, the truck sat in the driveway for over a month, accruing expenses daily. Moving is always stressful, but Mandy's experience took it to another level. Had she aligned her plans with astrological timing, she could have saved herself thousands of dollars and much less stress.

Despite facing numerous challenges, Mandy maintained her sense of humor, calling to exclaim, "The stars were absolutely right!" Needless to say, Mandy never doubted the power of astrological timing again. Today, she fully appreciates the importance of working with her planetary transits and alignments for optimal timing, rather than resisting them.

Using Astrology in my Coaching practice

Integrating astrology with life coaching offers clients a unique roadmap that bridges the mystical and practical aspects of personal development. The result is a comprehensive approach to self-improvement. Here's how I integrate astrology into my coaching practice:

1. Self-Discovery:

Astrology helps clients unearth their core strengths, challenges, and life purposes as encoded in their natal charts. This self-awareness serves as a foundation for personal growth and empowers the client to make more aligned choices.

2. Career and Vocational Guidance:

Astrology can reveal one's vocational aptitudes, potential career paths, and periods where career changes might be favorable. With this information, clients can align their career choices with their innate talents and external opportunities, crafting a career path that resonates deeply with their true selves.

3. Timing and Cycles:

Astrological transits and cycles provide insights into the timing of significant life events and transitions. By aligning actions with favorable cosmic phases, clients can navigate changes more easily and effectively.

4. Understanding Relationships:

By comparing and interpreting the synastries (relationship charts), I guide clients toward harmonious relationships. Understanding the astrological dynamics between people fosters empathy, improved communication, and mutual growth.

5. Overcoming Challenges:

Every astrological chart contains areas of tension and growth. Recognizing and addressing these areas equips clients to overcome personal and professional obstacles, transforming challenges into opportunities.

6. Life Transitions:

Astrological Insight: Major life transitions—such as moving, marriage, or career shifts are often reflected in one's astrological chart. By understanding the optimal timing for these changes, clients can make informed decisions, reducing stress and enhancing the likelihood of successful outcomes.

7. Setting Intentions:

Utilizing lunar cycles and planetary transits, I help clients set intentions and goals aligned with cosmic rhythms, maximizing the potential for success and personal transformation.

8. Emotional and Mental Well-being

We can identify periods of potential stress or emotional upheaval by examining planetary influences on emotional well-being. I assist clients in developing coping strategies tailored to these astrological insights, equipping them with tools to manage difficult times proactively.

A Transformative Approach.

Life coaching through the lens of astrology is not about predicting the future but rather empowering individuals to become active participants in their life journey. It's about recognizing innate potential and working diligently to achieve the desired outcomes. The stars may guide us, but it's our actions that define the journey.

Each client I work with teaches me something sacred about the human experience and the intricate web of destiny. My role is to be a catalyst, sparking the realization of their potential and helping them navigate life's complexities with greater clarity and confidence.

Conclusion:

My journey from an intrigued stargazer to an astrologer life coach is a testament to the power of following one's passion and the transformative integration of ancient wisdom with contemporary coaching. The cosmos holds answers, and through astrology, we can decode these celestial messages, merging them with practical coaching strategies to create a life of purpose, harmony, and fulfillment.

Guiding individuals through their celestial blueprints and witnessing their transformations is not merely a career but a calling. Just as the stars illuminate the night sky, my mission is to illuminate the paths of those seeking direction, helping them realize that they, too, can shine brightly in their unique constellations of life.

Are you ready to dive deeper into your astrological journey?

As a special thank you for reading this chapter, I'm offering a free 15-minute consultation call. This personalized session is a great opportunity for you to ask any questions and get a taste of how astrology coaching can help you understand and navigate your life better.

You can book your free call now by visiting my website: https://shop.marysastrology.com

You can also take advantage of this exclusive offer:

Get a 20% discount on your first full astrology session by using the code ASTRO20

Don't miss out on these opportunities to enhance your understanding and harness the power of astrology!

About Mary Trimble

Mary Trimble has over three decades of counseling expertise. As a life coach and astrologer, Mary has helped many individuals achieve transformative changes through her profound insights and intuitive guidance. Her passion for astrology began with a self-taught approach. Mary's unrelenting passion for astrology eventually led her to  formalize her education with the American Federation of Astrologers (AFA) and with renowned astrologer Robert Corre at The Forum on Astrology. Numerous eminent astrologers have contributed to Mary's education, and as a current member of the International Society for Astrological Research (ISAR), she remains dedicated to continually advancing and deepening her practice.

Inspired by motivational figures like Tony Robbins and Bob Proctor, Mary pursued life coaching to better guide her clients. Deciding the first step would be to employ a coach, she googled "Life coach," but unfortunately it wasn't a good fit. Despite her disappointing experience, she was determined to pursue a life coaching certification. Mary's prerequisite for training was an affordable online course and after extensive research, Mary chose Wainwright Global Institute for Professional Coaching, graduating in 2010. This fusion of astrology and life coaching allowed Mary to provide uniquely tailored guidance that resonated deeply with her clients, enabling profound personal growth and transformation.

"A Picture-Perfect Recipe" .... for Life

The Recipe will become divinely unique to YOU and only YOU

"Do What You Love First"

by Sian Lindemann

The truth be known, I stumbled into Life Coaching.

In fact, it was Barbara G. Wainwright who deliberately "tricked" me into participating.

Despite how or why I had become involved with Life Coaching, Life Coach Certification Training and a myriad of other classes and titles....

It has, by far, become one of the most penetrating and powerful experiences in my life.

It has been catalytic for my growth, my depth, my passion, my creativity, my delight, my laughter AND my rage.

And in the years since my initial involvement, we have serviced, trained and consulted with over 7,000 coaches worldwide.

And in the business in which I was most well-known, business development in the Fine Arts and subsequent sales, millions of dollars of fine art creations have been sold worldwide

HOWEVER, All Said, the simplest of outcomes is what is now my life, which is far more rewarding, and has offered the most contentment.

I have come to love, trust and participate in two things.

I do them, first.

I love COOKING and HORSES

I have come to know:

I love horses and always have them with me.

And if I am not in the environment to create extraordinary dining in my home, I do it wherever I am……

Those two things have brought me beauty, depth, richness, value, passion, artistry and LOVE.

Those are the ingredients.

The recipe is as follows…….as it pertains to my view on HOW to live a fulfilled and happy life.

At 67 years of age, it has all gotten VERY simple……

Through coaching, all the should haves, have fallen away.

These following 10 things allow my heart to beat fully.

One. Take Care of YOUR Body. There is nothing that you love to do, that you will be able to do, unless you care for the vehicle, first. Do whatever it takes to care, feed and nourish the body and find the best health care professionals to guide you.

Two. Do what you LOVE first. You'll find, often, that even as little as 5 minutes of doing what you love, first, will provide boundless energy and excitement for the rest of the tasks required in the 23 hours of the rest of the day.

Three. Choose to HELP others who WANT your help. The rest will watch, judge, smirk, and perhaps attempt to copy you. The ones who want your excellent expertise will thrive.

Four. Learn the difference between LOVE and LUST.

Lust will excite the senses. Use it to open yourself to the delight of your own creativity and the buzz of new ideas.

LOVE will tenderly envelope your soul to the deepest wellspring of self…. and so gorgeous it is. Make LOVE visible.

Five. Overdose on the discovery of your Calling. Never back up from it.

Trust your heart. Let it guide you, no matter what.

Six. Spend as much time in nature as you can.

Seven. Trust that GOD has your back. God is NOT a religion.

Eight. Revere, uplift, and tell your true friends how much they mean to you, always.

Nine. Honor your agreements

Ten. Have Fun, and if it isn't, make it be so…. or don't do it!!!

The ingredients will be your own.

The Recipe will also become divinely unique to YOU and only YOU.

It is, indeed, the very premise of coaching. We never tell you what to do.

In asking the right questions, we allow you to hear YOUR own answers, listen to your heart, and let your smile, and your action, radiate out into the world in a new and illuminated way.

Be YOURSELF. Experience the Difference

About Sian Lindemann

Sian Lindemann is 67 years young, and is an Artist and Human Being.

With over 50 years' experience, imparting financial viability to and for creatives, Sian knows a thing or two about choice.

Choose what you love, first!!!

Make it financially viable.

Live a life, by Design.

"Sian Design"

Where The Sky Is Born

Sian Lindemann CPC, CMC, CCC, CGLC, CSC, Artist, Mentor, All Round Creative Tornado, Business Development Specialist

"Do What You Love First"!

Don't know how to make your passion profitable?

Contact Me!

For over 50 years I have been assisting "the creative" to make money with their primary passion. Let me show you how!!!

Sian Lindemann CPC, CMC, CCC, CGLC, CSC

Artist and Human Being

505 542 9217

thelandofenchantmentsiandesign@gmail.com

Create a Fulfilling Life by Embracing Your Divine Purpose

"We all have something that we've gone through that rocks our world and awakens us to the reality that we are invincible spirits having a temporary human experience."

"Show Up for God, and God Will Show Up for You in Miraculous Ways"

by Barbara Wainwright

Living your divine purpose so that you can live a fulfilled life is really a choice. You have free-will to choose. You decide.

Many years ago, before I began my coaching career, I was searching for something that was fulfilling, and made a difference in the world.

I'm primarily a California girl, however at age 17, my family went to England for my father's work. I attended North Gloucester College of Technology and studied computer programming. I met my first husband there and by the time I was 19, we had our first baby girl.

At age 21, my husband, daughter and I left England to start a new life in California, and to be close to my family. Not long after we arrived, I began working as a computer operator and soon got pregnant with my son. Unfortunately, things didn't work out in my marriage and we divorced 9 months after my son was born. This was my first venture as a single parent with 2 kids, and a full-time job as a computer programmer.

11 years after my first divorce, I remarried and had 2 more children. During this time, I was still working in the software/tech industry. That marriage also failed and that is when I took a deep-dive into understanding people, behaviors, belief systems, psychology, and the resulting effects that trauma can have on a person's psyche. I was desperate to stop feeling "less than" and to find a loving, supportive relationship with a significant other.

I earned certifications in Crystal Healing, Pranic Healing, Hypnosis, Neuro-Linguistic Programming, and Intuitive Channeling. I became a Certified Spiritual Counselor. I read personal development books by M. Scott Peck, Patricia Evans, Melodie Beatty, Sylvia Browne, Gay Hendricks, Eckhart Tolle, Jane Roberts, and a host of other esteemed authors. I also attended meditation classes at Long Beach State University with Dr. Martin Feibert. The meditations were long, intense, and opened up a strong field of energy that I have carried with me ever since.

I had a voracious appetite for learning about life, and people. I joined a 12-step group called Codependence Anonymous and attended meetings for many years. It took me three years to find a sponsor, but when I did, I worked the steps and found that it was a very healing process. I was beginning to understand people and how they think. I began to feel safe in the world. I learned to listen and observe. I learned to pay attention to what people say, and then to observe them to see if they did what they said. I found that it is an important indicator of their personal integrity. Are they true to their word?

During this time, I earned a living as a consultant and supported my children by designing and developing software for various companies. As I was learning about people and growing my spiritual practice, I felt a yearning growing in my heart and soul. I knew there was something else that I was supposed to be doing besides designing systems and writing computer code, but I hadn't put my finger on it.

One day while sitting at my computer, I stumbled upon a website that described life coaching. Becoming a life coach felt like the answer immediately. I checked in with my inner-guidance; I prayed about it. The message I received was a huge "Yes". With confirmation that this was my divine path and purpose, I jumped into the coaching industry whole-heartedly. I booked a flight and flew to Canada to receive my coach training.

I fell in love with coaching, however, within a few years, I had the realization that most coach certification training programs were too expensive for the average person to take advantage of. Furthermore, the courses that were offered seemed to drag the training out over an extended period of time because the requirements for certification were arduous and were not based on a person's ability to coach. They were based on the hours they attended training. That just didn't make sense to me. I am very logical (which is a great attribute for a programmer/analyst).

Over time, I designed a step-by-step system of coaching, which can be used in any coaching niche and can be taught in only 16 hours. I have since designed an easy method to get clients, which has also been proven to work.

Fast forward to today. I now run Wainwright Global Institute of Professional Coaching (WGI) and through my company, we have certified well-over 6,000 professional coaches.

An independent researcher from Seattle Washington, followed WGI graduates for several years and created case studies proving that the coaching system provides transformation for clients. Subsequently, the WGI curriculum was accredited by the American Association of Colleges and Schools of Business (AACSB) through the Business Program at Seattle Pacific University. A University Graduate Level course in Leadership adopted my coaching curriculum to teach leaders and executives at BOEING how to coach as part of that leadership program.

Coaching is now widely accepted as an integral part of Leadership and Management and employees that have coaches are more engaged, more productive and tend to stay longer at their jobs when they are being coached.

After several years of leading WGI, I realized that my own life was in need of an adjustment. I had been working long hours and was still making time to get my kids to school and to their extracurricular activities. It made for a very long day. I decided to cut back on my business hours and to start taking some "me" time. It was a great decision.

To reduce my hours, I cut back on advertising. It is a time-consuming process to create and place ads and to follow-up and monitor to make sure they are working. For 10 years now, my company has been sustained by referrals and I am so grateful for every referral I have received.

As a single parent, and CEO of a company, I didn't have time to pursue a relationship. I was married to my work. When I cut back on my working hours, I now had the time and the willingness to explore a relationship. I experimented with a couple dating apps, however, I never went on a 2nd date with anyone I dated. It didn't seem like the timing was right.

Eventually, my children grew up and were no longer living at home. I'd never lived alone and didn't really want to. When I sold my house, I decided to move into a "room share" in a mansion. It seemed like an adventure! This was when I made my claim. "God, I am now ready for my "happily, forever after" relationship. That was it. I was ready. I didn't need to complicate things by putting parameters, or limitations on my request. "Happily, forever after" was all I needed! God knew my heart, my mind, my soul, my prayer.

Six months later, the landlord of the mansion requested that I go upstairs and meet a potential new tenant. I thought that was odd. I'd never "room shared" before so I didn't know I had any "say" in whether a new roommate would be accepted or not. I went upstairs and met the new roommate. Now I don't remember if anyone else was in the room or not. We looked into each other's eyes and said "Hello"; our eyes locked and we were immediately attracted and drawn to each other.

Thirty days later, we were a committed couple and I'm happy to say that our lives just keep getting better and better. We are both so grateful and feel so blessed that we met that fateful day.

That brings us to the present.

Since 2020, I have been the host of a podcast called "The Power of Now - A Guide to Spiritual Enlightenment with Gilda and Barbara". It is successful and it has been picked up by a radio station now. It is rewarding to know that our podcast is helping people to understand and integrate the spiritual works of Eckhart Tolle.

This book is the 4th anthology book that has been published with all the chapter contributions coming from Wainwright Global Certified Professional Coaches. After years of people telling me I should have a book, I decided that I could write a chapter! For years, I didn't think I had a "book" in me. In the last couple of years, I have made time to work on a book about spirituality. The working title is "The Six Stages of Spiritual Awakening". The chapters are Awakening: Becoming Conscious, Testing the Universal Truths, Practicing the Principles of Spirituality, Trusting the Principles, The Surrender of Your Will, Meditation and Prayer. My plan is to complete that book in the next 12 months or so.

My life experiences have influenced and created the person I am today. I love my life and all the beloved people that surround me. I feel blessed beyond my imagination and I am extremely grateful for everything that has happened; the good, the bad and the ugly, the inspiring, the uplifting, and the miraculous blessings.

I believe by sharing our strengths and weaknesses, that we help each other realize that we are all connected. We all have something that we've gone through that rocks our world and awakens us to the reality that we are invincible spirits having a temporary human experience. Our egos are threatened by just about everything. If we can get our egos in check, we can have an amazing human experience while we are here. And in the big scheme of things, we are only here for a blink of the eye.

You are a beloved child of God and your divine purpose is meant to be shared with the world. If you aren't living a life you love, fulfilling your purpose, right here, right now. I ask you, why not? What is stopping you? When will you give yourself permission to do what you are called to do? If not now, then when?

May God bless you in miraculous ways.

About Barbara Wainwright

Barbara Wainwright is Certified Master Life Coach and CEO of Wainwright Global, Barbara Wainwright is known as the most sought-after teacher in the coaching and self-empowerment industry. She is famous for training and certifying over 6,000 professional coaches worldwide since 2006 and for creating the "Wainwright Method of  Coaching", empowering individuals to actualize their life purpose, live inspired lives, and connect with their true passion.

Using her University Accredited curriculum, Barbara has trained employees at BOEING, Syracuse University, Washington University and more. She is an international speaker, author, and educator and this is her 4th published anthology book created with the collaboration of Wainwright Global Certified Professional Coaches.

Barbara hosts a Podcast entitled "The Power of Now - A Guide to Spiritual Enlightenment with Gilda and Barbara" currently with over 800,000 downloads. The podcast is now streaming on KPHRED.com and KAPY Radio.

Barbara has recorded over 60 Video Shorts in her YouTube series: "Show Up For God and God Will Show Up For You In Miraculous Ways."

Her free book entitled 10 Essential Things You Absolutely Must Know Before You Start Your Coaching Career is available at her website: WainwrightGlobal.com.

When Barbara's not spending time with her grandson, you will find her enjoying the beautiful environment of Newport Beach, California where she currently resides.

Barbara Wainwright, CPC®

CEO, Wainwright Global, Inc.

800-711-4346

Barbara@WainwrightGlobal.com

https://www.LifeCoachTrainingOnline.com